DAVID LINDSAY

by

Gary K. Wolfe

Starmont Reader's Guide 9

BORGO PRESS / WILDSIDE PRESS

www.wildsidepress.com

To my parents

Gary K. Wolfe is Dean of the College of Continuing Education at Roosevelt University and the author of *The Known and the Unknown: The Iconography of Science Fiction*, for which he received the J. Lloyd Eaton Award. He has published numerous essays and articles on science fiction and fantasy.

First Edition————June, 1982

Cover and title page design by Stephen E. Fabian Sr. & Jr.

copyright © 1982 by Starmont House

Library of Congress Cataloging in Publication Data

Wolfe, Gary K., 1946-
  David Lindsay.

  (Starmont reader's guide ; 10)
  Bibliography: p.
  Includes index.
  1. Lindsay, David, 1876-1945—Criticism and inter-
pretation.   I. Title.   II. Series: Starmont reader's
guides to contemporary science fiction and fantasy
authors ; 10.
PR6023.I58115Z96 1982   823'.914   81-21679
ISBN 0-89370-041-X   AACR2
Library of Congress Cataloging in Publication Data

CONTENTS

I

CHRONOLOGY OF LIFE AND WORKS

1878	David Lindsay born March 3 at Blackheath, a suburb of London.
1891	When David is 13, his father deserts the family.
c. 1898	Lindsay employed as a clerk in an insurance firm.
c.1914–16	Military service in the British Grenadiers.
1916	Marries wife Jacqueline and moves to a cliffside house on the ocean in St. Columb Minor, Cornwall.
1919	April: Begins composition of *A Voyage to Arcturus.*
1920	Completes *A Voyage to Arcturus* in March. The novel is accepted by Methuen, but some 15,000 words are cut from the text. The published novel sells only 596 copies.
1921	Completes *The Haunted Woman* in April, but the novel is declined by Methuen. Lindsay cuts 20,000 words, and the London *Daily News* accepts the novel for serialization.
1921	August: Begins work on third novel, *Sphinx.*
1921	October: Methuen reconsiders and accepts *The Haunted Woman.*
1922	February: *The Haunted Woman* published by Methuen to slow sales. March: finishes first draft of *Sphinx.* May: *Sphinx* declined by three publishers. June-July: Begins work on *The Ancient Tragedy*, a novel later to be reworked as *Devil's Tor.*
1923	April: An agent places *Sphinx* with John Long, a publisher of popular genre fiction. May: completes only "commercial" novel, *The Adventures of M. de Mailly.* October: finishes draft of *The Ancient Tragedy.*
1923–25	*M. de Mailly* and *Ancient Tragedy* rejected by several publishers.
1924	*The Violet Apple* written between February and July; rejected by John Long.
1925	Lindsay begins revisions on *The Violet Apple.* A Sept. 16 letter from novelist L. H. Myers begins a curious friendship and encourages Lindsay to continue writing.
1926	February: *M. de Mailly* finally published, by Andrew Melrose. Lindsay completes revision of *The Violet Apple.*
1927	*M. de Mailly*, retitled *Blade for Sale*, becomes Lindsay's first book published in the United States.
1928	Lindsay begins *Devil's Tor*, a reworking of *The Ancient Tragedy.* Moves from Cornwall to Ferring, Sussex. At Christmas, writes a fairy play (now lost) for his daughters.

1931	L. H. Myers sends *Devil's Tor* to Putnam's.
1932	Putnam accepts *Devil's Tor* in January, advances Lindsay 50 pounds. *Devil's Tor* is the last of Lindsay's books to be published in his lifetime. Despite some favorable notices, the novel sells only 650 copies.
	June-Sept.: Lindsay, in financial difficulty, fails repeatedly to persuade Putnam to reissue *Arcturus*.
c. 1933–39	Lindsay works on his last novel, *The Witch*. It is rejected by publishers repeatedly.
c. 1938–39	Family forced to move to Brighton and take in boarders.
1939–45	Lindsay grows increasingly reclusive and despondent over the war and his own failures.
1945	On June 6, Lindsay dies, mainly from a tooth infection, but partly as the result of a shock received when a bomb struck his house in Brighton. The bomb did not explode, but collapsed the ceiling of Lindsay's bathroom while Lindsay was in his bath.
1946	Gollancz reissues *Arcturus*.
1963	Gollancz reissues *Arcturus* again, and the first United States edition is published by Macmillan, with an introduction by Loren Eiseley.
1968	Ballantine (U.S.) issues first paperback of *Arcturus*. Reprinted 1973.
1969	William Holloway, a student filmmaker, produces a short experimental film based on *A Voyage to Arcturus*.
1970	Colin Wilson, J. B. Pick and E. H. Visiak publish the first book on Lindsay, *The Strange Genius of David Lindsay* (London: John Baker).
1975	*The Violet Apple* and *The Witch*, edited by J. B. Pick, are published in a single volume (Chicago: Chicago Review Press), later reprinted in London by Sidgwick & Jackson.
1981	Bernard Sellin's *The Life and Works of David Lindsay*, translated by Kenneth Gunell, is published by Cambridge University Press.

II

LIFE, INFLUENCE, AND REPUTATION

On October 29, 1944, C. S. Lewis, the Christian apologist best known in science-fiction circles for his trilogy *Out of the Silent Planet, Perelandra,* and *That Hideous Strength*—each of which takes place on a different planet—wrote in a letter to Charles Brady:

> The real father of my planet books is David Lindsay's *Voyage to Arcturus,* which you will also revel in if you don't know it. I had grown up on Wells's stories of that kind; it was Lindsay who first gave me the idea that the "scientifiction" appeal could be combined with the "supernatural" appeal.[1]

Shortly thereafter, in a lecture before the Merton College undergraduate literary society at Oxford, Lewis introduced Lindsay to a somewhat wider audience. Speaking of stories in which the ominous setting prepares the reader for horrors that are sometimes not adequately delivered, Lewis listed a few authors who really *do* deliver, among them Homer and Walter de la Mare. "But perhaps the most remarkable achievement in this kind," Lewis continued, "is that of Mr. David Lindsay's *A Voyage to Arcturus.*" He added:

> There is no recipe for writing of this kind. But part of the secret is that the author (like Kafka) is recording a lived dialectic. His Tormance is a region of the spirit. He is the first writer to discover what 'other planets' are really good for in fiction. No merely physical strangeness or merely spatial distance will realize that idea of otherness which is what we are always trying to grasp in a story about voyaging through space: you must go into another dimension. To construct plausible and moving 'other worlds' you must draw on the only real 'other world' we know, that of the spirit.[2]

Whether or not Lewis had any direct or deliberate impact on it, interest in David Lindsay and his masterpiece, *A Voyage to Arcturus,* began slowly to grow from about this time. The copy of *A Voyage to Arcturus* that Lewis had read sometime in the 1930s was probably one of only 596 copies that the book sold after it was first published in 1920. Perhaps it was sheer chance that put this almost forgotten novel into Lewis's hands, or perhaps Lewis had heard something of it from the small but persistent rumors of its strangeness and power that had kept the book's reputation alive despite its almost total lack of commercial success. It may have been these rumors, too, that prompted the English publisher Victor Gollancz to reissue *A Voyage to Arcturus* for the first time in 1946. This allowed the book to reach a still wider audience, and its reputation continued to grow. In 1963, Gollancz reissued the book again, as part of a series called "Rare Works of Imaginative Fiction." By now the publisher could advertise on the dust jacket that *A Voyage to Arcturus* had become "one of the most famous 'underground' books of the century." That same year an American publisher, Macmillan, started a series called "Macmillan's Library of Science-Fiction Classics" and included in the series the first American edition of *A Voyage to Arcturus*, at the same time first attaching the label "science-fiction" to the book. Loren Eiseley, the naturalist, wrote an earnest if often erroneous introduction, and the book began for the first time to reach an American audience. Among the American readers was Betty Ballantine of Ballantine Books, who was looking for classics of fantastic literature to reprint in the wake of her earlier successes with works of J. R. R. Tolkien, E. R. Eddison, and Mervyn Peake. In November of 1968, *A Voyage to Arcturus* became the thirteenth work published in this series, and for the first time saw the light of day as a mass-market paperback. It soon became a staple of college courses in fantastic literature and was reprinted by Ballantine again in April of 1973. In 1977, Gregg Press issued a hardbound reprint of the first edition. By now, the book had become widely discussed in science-fiction circles. Harlan Ellison read it and enjoyed it "very much," and Philip José Farmer once said *A Voyage to Arcturus* was "a seminal book for me." In 1977, Robert Scholes and Eric Rabkin discussed the novel as one of "ten representative novels" of science-fiction in their *Science-Fiction: History, Science, Vision* (Oxford University Press).

Meanwhile, in England, Lindsay's reputation continued to spread. In addition to C. S. Lewis's published acknowledgment of the influence of *A Voyage to Arcturus*, Colin Wilson discovered the book and included a long essay on it in his 1966 collection *Eagle and Earwig*. Gollancz reissued another Lindsay novel, *The Haunted Woman*, in 1964, the same year that the Scottish novelist J. B. Pick published one of the first critical assessments of Lindsay in *Studies in Scottish Literature*. Between 1966 and 1968, Wilson, Pick, and Lindsay's surviving friend E. H. Visiak began collaborating on a book-length study of Lindsay, which appeared as *The Strange Genius of David Lindsay* in 1970. Pick later edited Lindsay's two unpublished novels, *The Violet Apple* and *The Witch*, for a one-volume hardbound edition published by the Chicago Review Press in 1976. Lindsay, it seems, had finally arrived.

All of this would undoubtedly seem ironic to the strange, reclusive man whose only reputation during his lifetime was that of a "conspicuously unsalable author."[3] At the time C. S. Lewis wrote to his friend Brady in 1944 about the influence *A Voyage to Arcturus* had had on him, Lindsay was still alive and living in Brighton, an embittered old man increasingly depressed about the war and his own failure to succeed as a writer. None of his books had been in print for more than a decade, two of them had never found a publisher, and Lindsay had even failed in repeated attempts to get *A Voyage to Arcturus* reprinted and raise much-needed money. Within nine months he would be dead at the age of 67, less than a year before the first Gollancz reprint of *A Voyage to Arcturus*.

In Lindsay's last novel, *The Witch*, he had written about one of his characters, "Some devil was in it that he should write his books, read by few, comprehended by fewer, wanted by none!"[4] It is likely that Lindsay was thinking of his own literary career, which did not begin until he was in his forties and consisted of a series of disasters spanning about twelve years, from 1920 to 1932. Never quite able to master a comfortable style or to find a widely accessible means of expressing his complex but very rigorous philosophical ideas, Lindsay tried several genres and wrote novels of varying lengths, but somehow each work seemed less successful than the last. He moved from a work that at first glance appeared to be an inter-planetary romance (*A Voyage to Arcturus*) to one that looked like a ghost-story (*The Haunted Woman*) to an historical swashbuckler (*The Adventures of M. de Mailly*), but none of these, with the exception of *A Voyage to Arcturus*, seemed quite able to accommodate his vision, and it is likely that the failure of *A Voyage to Arcturus* prompted him to try these other forms in the hopes of reaching the audience that continually eluded him. He once told Victor Gollancz, "Somewhere in the world, someone will be reading a book of mine every year."[5] This is certainly true today, but the statement sounds like highly uncharacteristic optimism for an author whose career had been as invisible as Lindsay's was during his own life.

Lindsay was born March 3, 1878 at Blackheath in Scotland.[6] Not much is know about his early life, but by the turn of the century, he was employed as a clerk in an insurance firm owned by Lloyd's of London. Despite the offer of a scholarship, he never attended a university, and this may account for the somewhat eclectic and idiosyncratic reading that influenced Lindsay as he was working on *A Voyage to Arcturus* and his other books. According to Lindsay's own account, he had begun working out the ideas that were to become *A Voyage to Arcturus* as early as 1910. He served in the British Grenadiers during the war, never leaving England, and in 1916 married his wife Jacqueline and moved to a cliffside house on the ocean at St. Columb Minor in Cornwall. Surrounded by this rugged landscape, he began writing *A Voyage to Arcturus* in April of 1919 and completed it the following March. Robert Lynd, a reader for the publishing firm of Methuen, was impressed enough by the work to accept it for publication, but this good news was tempered by the first of Lindsay's many disappointments in dealing with publishers: some 15,000 words had to be cut before the novel could be published. Those passages are now lost. Still, the prospect of a literary career begun this late in life must have been encouraging to Lindsay and his wife—at least until the sales figures on *A Voyage to Arcturus* revealed that, out of a press run of 1430 copies, only 596 were sold.

But by now Lindsay was writing in earnest, and he completed his second novel, *The Haunted Woman*, in April of 1921. This time Methuen declined to publish it at all, however, and Lindsay again set about making cuts—this time about 20,000 words—and eventually sold it for serialization to a newspaper. Later that year, Methuen reconsidered the novel and accepted it for publication. By now, Lindsay had already started a third novel, *Sphinx*. But when *The Haunted Woman* appeared in February of 1922, sales were again disappointing, and *Sphinx*, completed the following month, was declined by three publishers, including the newspaper that had serialized *The Haunted Woman*. Nevertheless, Lindsay began work on a fourth novel, which he called *The Ancient Tragedy*, and a fifth, *The Adventures of M. de Mailly.*

In 1923, Lindsay finally turned to the services of a literary agent to help get his books into print, and the agent did indeed find a publisher for *Sphinx* in April of that year. But both *The Ancient Tragedy* and *M. de Mailly* were rejected by a series of publishers over the next several years. Lindsay's good luck was indeed short-lived, but he continued to write, completing *The Violet Apple* between February and July of 1924. *The Violet Apple* would never see print during Lindsay's lifetime.

But Lindsay was not entirely without encouragement during this period. He had begun to hear from a few people who had read and been impressed by *A Voyage to Arcturus,* and one of these people was L. H. Myers, a novelist scarcely as well known as Lindsay today, but at the time somewhat more successful. Myers wrote to Lindsay on September 16, 1925, beginning a curious and somewhat uncomfortable friendship that nevertheless gained Lindsay a valuable advocate in trying to publish his manuscripts. And in 1926, a publisher finally accepted *M. de Mailly,* a complex historical romance that is probably Lindsay's most readable book. *M. de Mailly* even did well enough to be picked up by an American publisher, who issued it as *Blade for Sale* in 1927.

The Ancient Tragedy still could not find a publisher, however, and in 1928 Lindsay began to completely rework it under the new title, *Devil's Tor.* Later he also moved from Cornwall to Ferring in Sussex. Even cut down from *The Ancient Tragedy, Devil's Tor* was by far the longest of Lindsay's books so far—487 pages in its published edition—and might never have seen print, either, had it not been for the influence of Myers, who sent it to Putnam's in 1931. In January of 1932, Putnam's accepted the manuscript and advanced Lindsay 50 pounds—hardly enough to alleviate the increasing financial difficulties that Lindsay found himself in by now. The investments resulting from a lump-sum payment that Lindsay had received when he left his insurance firm were no longer sufficient to sustain the genteel literary life that Lindsay had wanted for himself, and a friend of Lindsay's, Robert Barnes, even recalled coming upon Lindsay one night digging up the cinder path in his garden to use as fuel to heat the house. Much of Lindsay's future, in more ways than one, seemed to be invested in the success of *Devil's Tor.* The novel appeared in April of 1932, and Lindsay had reason to be encouraged. The publisher wrote to Lindsay that he considered the work a "classic" that "has a long life before it."[7] A number of well-known writers (or later to be well-known) wrote reviews, many of which were favorable. Rebecca West called it "an excellent specimen of its kind"; L. P. Hartley praised Lindsay's "complete originality of mind and great intensity of feeling"; Hugh l'Anson Fausset called it a "vast, formidable, and overpowering book." Other reviews were not so encouraging, however: J. B. Priestly called the novel "woefully cumbersome, turgid, and unconvincing," and H. E. Bates described it as "a heavy, woolly piece of work."[8] In the end, the novel sold only 650 copies, only 54 more than *A Voyage to Arcturus* had sold a dozen years earlier.

Throughout the summer of 1932, Lindsay tried to persuade Putnam's to reissue *A Voyage to Arcturus*, but the poor sales of *Devil's Tor* discouraged the publisher from taking another risk. Depressed and vastly discouraged, Lindsay nevertheless set to work on his final novel, *The Witch*, which he hoped would encompass the apparently contradictory philosophical positions expressed in *A Voyage to Arcturus* and *Devil's Tor*. He worked slowly and meticulously, almost obsessively, on this novel throughout the thirties, but he was never able to find a publisher for it. Growing financial strains forced the family to move to Brighton before the war and take in boarders, and during the war years, Lindsay grew increasingly reclusive and despondent. His death came in a bizarre and almost absurdly comic way: during the bombardment of England, a bomb damaged Lindsay's house while Lindsay was taking a bath in his upstairs bathroom. The bomb did not explode, but the ceiling to the bathroom collapsed, and the shock may have contributed to Lindsay's already deteriorating health. His death on June 6, 1945 apparently was actually the result of blood poisoning that resulted from a severe tooth infection.

After Lindsay's death, Jacqueline Lindsay sold much of his library, making it difficult for scholars to determine with any great accuracy what his reading habits may have been or what direct influences might be present in his writing. We do know that he was fond of German metaphysics, the Norse sagas, historical works dealing with the Roman Empire, and personal memoirs of the eighteenth century (the latter of which almost certainly provided some of the background material for *The Adventures of M. de Mailly*). Of the authors that we know to have been represented in his library, those of particular interest include Goethe, Nietzsche, Schopenhauer, Emerson, Robert Louis Stevenson, Rider Haggard, and F. Max Muller's *Three Lectures on Vedanta Philosophy*. But to regard these works as in any sense "sources" for the phenomenal inventiveness of such works as *A Voyage to Arcturus* would be misleading, for even in cases in which names or concepts are borrowed from earlier writers, Lindsay almost invariably altered the material in such a way as to make the detection of the original meanings treacherous at best.

But a few books and authors can be fairly said to have been seminal to Lindsay's thought. Among these are the Icelandic Eddas, which provided some of the imagery and nomenclature of *Arcturus*; Nietzsche and Schopenhauer, both of whose thought permeates Lindsay's philosophical system as it evolved through his several novels; and the nineteenth-century Scottish novelist and fantasist George MacDonald, whose *Phantastes* and *Lilith* may well have given Lindsay the idea for the basic ideational structure of *Arcturus*. In fact, Lindsay once told his friend E. H. Visiak that George MacDonald had been his greatest influence.[9]

MacDonald (1824-1905) was a Scottish minister and novelist best known today for his children's fantasies, such as *At the Back of the North Wind*, *The Princess and the Goblin*, and "The Golden Key," though in his own time MacDonald's many romances of Scottish life were widely read. In reference to Lindsay, however, two of MacDonald's works seem particularly important: *Phantastes* (1858) and *Lilith* (1895). With these two works, one written near the beginning of his career and the other near the end, MacDonald pioneered a form of symbolic fantasy that offered the richness of imagery of allegory without the restraining ideological structures associated with that form. Like Lindsay, MacDonald was fond of the German romantic fairy tales known as *Märchen*, but in his adult fantasies MacDonald refined and developed the *Märchen* into a form that had much of the internal consistency and power of myth. MacDonald's ideology may not have been the same as Lindsay's, but there is much to suggest that the essential structures and patterns of imagery laid out by MacDonald provided Lindsay with just the sort of fictional guise he was looking for to explore his philosophical notions.

This essential structure, as first developed by MacDonald and later adapted by Lindsay (and through Lindsay by still later writers such as C. S. Lewis), can almost be expressed as a formula narrative: a character with no particular heroic qualities is dissatisfied with the illusory nature of "reality" and is lured by a mysterious tutelary figure into another world, where reality is much more fluid and where illusions can be stripped away. On the surface, this other world resembles the landscape of romance: it is predominantly rural, and the characters who inhabit it seem clearly good or evil. But none of the characters are quite what they seem; "good" characters may turn out to be evil, and vice versa. The protagonist, coming under the successive influence of a number of such characters in his quest to find his way back to "reality," gradually realizes that none of the realities he encounters are absolute and that merely returning home will not sufficiently answer his deepening questions about the nature of reality. As he becomes progressively stripped of his illusions, he becomes increasingly aware of the power of an antagonist, a master of illusion, who seeks to keep him from the truth. On occasion, the tutelary figure saves the protagonist from being seduced by this master of illusion, but as the protagonist gains strength as he loses his illusions, he himself becomes more of an heroic and tutelary figure, helping to guide others through this strange world. At the end of his quest, the emerging hero, through an act of supreme pain and self-sacrifice—a form of death, in fact—achieves a vision of his own true reality, undergoes a transformation, and returns to the world of his origin. This is essentially the narrative of MacDonald's *Phantastes* and *Lilith* and Lindsay's *A Voyage to Arcturus*.

The imagery with which MacDonald portrays the other world—with predominant images of water, light, shadow, towers, the underworld, and crystal—is also reflected in Lindsay's work. The notion of both the tutelary figure and the antagonist each appearing in a number of guises is also common to both writers, as is the central notion that the reality somehow resides within the protagonist himself—that there is no reality outside the self. There is much to suggest that *A Voyage to Arcturus* would not be the book it is had it not been for the influence of MacDonald, and one passage from *Phantastes* even seems to suggest the central image of *A Voyage to Arcturus*: "No shining belt or gleaming moon," writes MacDonald, "no red and green glory in a self-encircling twin star, but has a relation with the hidden things of man's soul, and, it may be, with the secret history of his body as well."[10]

If MacDonald is one of the few literary influences we can detect on Lindsay, Lindsay's own influence on later writers is equally hard to measure. As we have already seen, C. S. Lewis credited Lindsay with the inspiration for his famous "space trilogy" (and not coincidentally elsewhere wrote that George MacDonald "had done more to me than any other writer"[11]), and we may infer from this that a number of later religious fantasies influenced by Lewis are thus also indirectly influenced by Lindsay. But since Lindsay wrote an odd kind of philosophical fantasy not really at all like science-fiction, it is difficult to find works that fall solidly within his tradition—and not all of the ones that do are works of science-fiction or fantasy. Many of Lindsay's ideas, for example, can be seen in an historical novel by the Scottish novelist J. B. Pick, *The Last Valley,* and some of Colin Wilson's odd and fantastic novels show a decided influence of Lindsay (in one, he even appropriates the character name "Saltfleet" from Lindsay's *Devil's Tor*). Of science-fiction writers, a great many seem to have read and been impressed by Lindsay—Philip José Farmer, Gordon Dickson, and Harlan Ellison, among others—and one can occasionally catch glimpses of a Lindsayesque vision in the later works of each of these writers. Perhaps the modern science-fiction work that most captures the spirit of Lindsay, however, and that most nearly approaches a "science-fictional" equivalent of the sort of thing Lindsay was doing in *A Voyage to Arcturus*, is Robert Silverberg's *Son of Man* (1971), which borrows even some of the exact imagery of the alien landscape from Lindsay's Tormance in *A Voyage to Arcturus*. It seems certain that as Lindsay continues to be widely taught in college classes dealing with fantastic literature (and *A Voyage to Arcturus* is certainly one of the most often-taught books in such classes), his influence will continue to spread, and interest will continue to grow in his lesser works, his ideas, and his strange and tragic career.

Notes

1. W. H. Lewis, ed., *Letters of C. S. Lewis* (London: Bles, 1966), p. 205.
2. Reprinted as "On Stories," in *Of Other Worlds: Essays and Stories,* ed. Walter Hooper (New York: Harcourt, Brace, & World, 1962), p. 12.
3. *Times Literary Supplement*, 20 November 1970, p. 1346.
4. *The Witch*, ms. p. 5.
5. Quoted in Lin Carter, *Imaginary Worlds* (New York: Ballantine, 1973), p. 94.
6. Most of the information on Lindsay's life is taken from Colin Wilson, E. H. Visiak, and J. B. Pick, *The Strange Genius of David Lindsay* (London: Baker, 1970), and from personal letters from Visiak and Pick.
7. Wilson, et al., p. 24.
8. Ibid., pp. 24-27.
9. Personal letter to the author from E. H. Visiak, 26 June 1970.
10. George MacDonald, *Phantastes and Lilith* (Grand Rapids: Eerdmans, 1964), p. 83.
11. C. S. Lewis, *Surprised by Joy* (New York: Harcourt, Brace, & World, 1966), p. 213.

III

A VOYAGE TO ARCTURUS

David Lindsay's major work, *A Voyage to Arcturus*, is surely among the most remarkable works of philosophical fiction of the twentieth century—but also, on first reading, one of the most puzzling. The reader who feels initially lost in the bizarre and philosophically dense landscape Lindsay creates should not feel alone, for the reviews of the book in its various editions are a testimony to the unflinching demands the book makes on readers and on the difficulty many readers have in dealing with these demands. The reviewer for the London *Times Literary Supplement* in 1920 (the year *A Voyage to Arcturus* was first published) compared it to Baudelaire and Poe, suspected it probably was an allegory of some sort, but declaimed its "uniform unwholesomeness."[1] But a 1963 reviewer for the same publication reacted enthusiastically to the reprint that year: "The book is not allegory but vision," this reviewer remarks, and speaks of the "remarkable profundity and coherence of the vision. The message is more likely to repel the casual reader than to attract him."[2] American reviews have not been much more consistent. *Book Week* called it a "spiritual allegory" too obscure to be of much value, while Brigid Brophy in *The New Statesman* complained of "bathetic ineptitudes" and suggested that what passed for metaphysics in the book was merely window dressing to disguise Lindsay's morbid interest in sex, concluding that the aesthetic value of the book was "of the same order as an embryo pickled in a bottle." (Lindsay *was* interested in sex, as we shall see, but the nature of his interest proved to be quite complex and thoughtful.) The *Library Journal* reviewer inaccurately recounted the plot, turning it into an almost unrecognizable adventure in which the central character must "constantly be on guard to protect himself from the invisible voices seeking to do him harm and to take advantage of those who will befriend him."[3] Kingsley Amis in the *New York Times Book Review* complained of "cheapjack marvels," suspected a religious allegory, and suggested that any such allegory should subscribe to "some great public myth," such as Christianity. "Without such underpinning it will fall, as here, into whimsey, into mere dream."[4] A more sympathetic approach is taken by poet and Renaissance scholar John Hollander in a brief but interesting review for the *New York Review of Books*. *A Voyage to Arcturus* begins, writes Hollander, as a kind of "fantasy kitsch," but soon develops into "a rather moving heroic poem, a prose romance deeply rooted in an English poetic tradition embracing Spenser, Milton, and the Romantics." Of the romantics, Hollander specifically invokes William Blake and Percy Shelley, regarding Lindsay's imaginary planet Tormance as derivative of both poets, but still "an original mythical landscape, loosely allegorizing states of human consciousness rather than ethical abstractions," as is the case with Charles Williams.

Lindsay's conclusion, he notes, is "far from being a traditional Christian one."[5] E. H. Visiak, however, an old friend of Lindsay's, has repeatedly maintained that the book is indeed Christian, that it is allegorical, and that Lindsay's figure of Crystalman is akin in a great many respects to Milton's Satan.[6] Muspel is therefore God, Visiak elsewhere argues, and Krag fulfills the role of the redeemer.[7] Visiak is himself a Milton scholar, and supports his arguments interestingly from the point of view of *Paradise Lost,* but he finds it necessary to ignore a great deal of *A Voyage to Arcturus* to make his position seem convincing.

One of the more interesting recent reactions to Lindsay's work is expressed by yet another *Time's Literary Supplement* reviewer, in writing on the Pick-Wilson-Visiak study, *The Strange Genius of David Lindsay.* This reviewer is perhaps more exemplary of contemporary attitudes toward Lindsay (the review is one of the first written of his work following the "boom" in fantasy publishing and study in the late sixties) in complaining of the author's "sticky" prose and apparently anti-literary bias. Even Lindsay's best work, he concludes, "is rather like an uncleaned copy of a Hieronymus Bosch original by a mediocre pupil of his school."[8]

Such widely varying reactions would in themselves indicate that the book possesses the quality that we have already described in C. S. Lewis's terms as myth, or story. But beyond the engrossing quality of the narrative, I would argue, there is in *A Voyage to Arcturus* a deliberate and detailed exposition of a specific philosophical system or attitude that is far more existential than Christian, more ascetic than romantic. The bases of this system are Lindsay's own, but it nevertheless seems worthwhile to regard briefly some of the literary and philosophical antecedents of *A Voyage to Arcturus,* although such a discussion can be at best fragmentary and suggestive. We have already noted (in Chapter One) the debt Lindsay owed to George MacDonald, but while MacDonald may have provided Lindsay with some ideas for the overall structure for a philosophical-symbolic fantasy and probably influenced his choice of imagery as well, there is much to suggest that the two men were of radically different temperaments, and that MacDonald's view of man and nature, though in some ways similar, cannot account for the complexities of Lindsay's philosophy. We have also noted Lindsay's fondness for the Norse sagas, and the images and terminology that he borrowed from these sources will soon become apparent. But the reality-principles that lie at the heart of Lindsay's system of thought probably owe more to Nietzsche and Schopenhauer than to any writers of fiction or fantasy. And there can be little doubt that Lindsay's notion of reality, stripped of all illusions, is one of the major keys to his thinking. " 'The first preliminary for all metaphysical thinking,' " he wrote in his notebooks, " 'is to produce within oneself the sense of *reality.*' "[9]

In Schopenhauer, the perceptual world exists as a projection of the will, which is a unity in every aspect of nature, differing from one natural object to the next (e.g., from plant—or crystal—to animal) only in the degree of its objectification. The higher grades of objectification—the individuality and consciousness of humans—are what concern Lindsay primarily in

A Voyage to Arcturus, but no aspect of his imagined landscape is without this suggestion of will. Like Schopenhauer in *The World as Will and Idea,* Lindsay believed that such forms of natural appearance are all illusory; matter is only permanent in the perceived world, and matter is only will perceived. Form "changes really every moment, and can only maintain itself so long as it clings as a parasite to matter."[10] Thus the entire perceived world is illusory, and such illusion is the source of apparent human happiness. "Every immoderate joy," writes Schopenhauer, "always rests on the delusion that one has found in life what can never be found there—lasting satisfaction of the harassing desires and cares, which are constantly breeding new ones. From every particular delusion of this kind one must inevitably be brought back later...."[11] And what brings us back, essentially, is pain. Pain alone has positive value, for pleasure and comfort can be perceived only in terms of the absence of pain. Hence we are furthest removed from reality when we are most comfortable. In *A Voyage to Arcturus* the character Krag, who in some sense represents a reality principle for Maskull and who generally fills the role of the hero's tutelary advocate (the role filled most often by the wise woman figure in MacDonald), is finally revealed to be a personification of what we know on earth as pain.[12]

This inadequate and therefore necessarily somewhat inaccurate representation of Schopenhauer's views is hardly sufficient to allow us to attempt to reconstruct the philosophical system that Lindsay was developing throughout his writing career (and in any event, such an attempt would be futile without access to Lindsay's notebooks), but it does provide a framework with which to begin a discussion of the philosophical bases of *A Voyage to Arcturus,* during which I hope to point out more specific literary relations between Lindsay and Schopenhauer and perhaps the earlier German romantics. In one important respect, however, Lindsay goes beyond Schopenhauer, for the nothingness that is the basis of reality and the final goal of Schopenhauerian logic and metaphysics is shown in *A Voyage to Arcturus* to be but the final illusion of Crystalman. There is another world beyond this nothingness, Lindsay seems to suggest, a world that is essentially ineffable and to which this nothingness is but a bridge. This is perhaps a somewhat more visionary outlook than is permitted by the system of Schopenhauer, and it may reflect Lindsay's reading of Vedanta philosophy. In Western literature, this calls to mind the tradition of *via negationis,* or the search for God by the stripping away of veils of illusion, and which, at least for purposes of this discussion, might be exemplified by the fourteenth-century English treatise *The Cloud of Unknowing.* In this work, as in *A Voyage to Arcturus,* all the faculties of perception—the senses, imagination, reason, intellect—stand between man and the Divine Spirit and in fact bombard man with various illusions. Only by minimizing the function of these faculties (but not by falling into passivity) can man approach the state of nonbeing that is a prerequisite to union with God.[13] This unknown God, which is beyond nothingness, is more closely related to Lindsay's Muspel than is Schopenhauer's state of nonbeing, although it is very possible that Lindsay found Schopenhauer more congenial to his own personality than the anonymous author ot *The Cloud of Unknowing*—and, as we shall see, Lindsay's own reading of Schopenhauer demanded that this state of nonbeing be equated with Muspel.

A third system of thought related to Lindsay, but more useful as a tool of interpretation than as a specific literary relation, is the myth of the hero, especially as interpreted in Jungian psychology as a metaphor of individuation. In the strictest mythical sense, *A Voyage to Arcturus* details the stages of the birth of the hero as described by Erich Neumann—overcoming and destroying aspects of the Great Mother and the Great Father in order to arrive at self-knowledge—and it is revealing that, according to Neumann, pain and discomfort are among the earliest and most essential factors to signal this process,[14] but it does seem rather unlikely that Lindsay was consciously aware of this particular mythic-psychological structure in more than a generic sense. This aspect of Lindsay, while an important one, deserves fuller consideration than the primarily literary scope of this study allows, and is perhaps best left to professional myth critics (who should have a veritable field day with *A Voyage to Arcturus* once they discover it).

What, then, is the effect of this difficult, savage, often very clumsy book, at first appearance mere inept science-fiction, upon the reader approaching it for the very first time? He will, for one thing, encounter an almost "pulpish" beginning that involves a seance, an apparent murder, and an interplanetary journey. He will find a cast of mostly unpleasant and unattractive characters, often presented in alienated and distrustful relationships with one another, and he is apt not to care greatly what happens to any of them. (Perhaps to avoid sentimentality, perhaps merely because of stylistic failings, Lindsay keeps the distance between reader and character at a maximum.) Philosophical pretensions become apparent the moment the hero arrives on the planet Tormance: he meets a genuinely attractive character named Joiwind and begins to learn the nature and value of the principle of self-sacrifice. But within another thirty or forty pages, Joiwind is left behind, the principle of self-sacrifice brought into serious question and finally rejected, and a whole new moral order introduced. At worst, the effect is annoying and perplexing; at best, it jars the reader out of his assumptions about expectation and fulfillment, about the often monistic nature of fantasy worlds, even about the nature of perceived reality and the validity of conventional values. C. S. Lewis describes the effect thus:

> Unaided by any special skill or even any sound taste in language, the author leads us up a stair of unpredictables. In each chapter we think we have found his final position; each time we are utterly mistaken. He builds whole worlds of imagery and passion, any one of which would have served another writer for a whole book, only to pull each of them to pieces and pour scorn on it.[15]

The careful reader thus develops the habit of distrusting virtually everything that is thrown at him and may despair of ever discovering what the author's own position really is. This is not an unreasonable despair; Lindsay's position is by his own admission undiscoverable. The entire world of his experience, he writes in his notebooks, is " 'rotten with illusion. Behind this sham world lies the real, tremendous, and awful Muspel-world, which knows neither will, nor Unity, nor Individuals: that is to say, an inconceivable world.' "[16]

Such a literary structure calls to mind the quotation from Novalis that MacDonald had used as an epigraph for *Phantastes,* in which Novalis speaks of narratives without coherence (*Zusammenhang*) that work by means of association, like dreams, and whose final effect is like music.[17] (Lindsay was also a passionate lover of music, especially Beethoven, and it is not outside the realm of possibility that he might have entertained the notion of musical structures for his fictions.) *A Voyage to Arcturus* is not without coherence, but its initial effect upon the reader depends more upon qualities of association than upon qualities of intellectual comprehension. Here again the difficulty may lie partly with the form of symbolic fantasy and with readers accustomed to the conventions of the novel or the romance. Rebecca West, in a review of Lindsay's later novel, *Devil's Tor*, defines the problem thus:

> Here is a case when the modern novel, so inveterately kind in its demands on the human attention, has incapacitated the novel reader from making an effort which is necessary if the novelist is to make his legitimate effect.[18]

This may be one reason why Lindsay has never acquired a wider audience, but the fact is that Lindsay does after all have severe limitations as a writer, as indicated to some extent by his attempts at more conventional techniques of the novel in a book like *The Haunted Woman.* What complicates the problem of Lindsay's style is that it is very easy to mistake his strengths for his weaknesses, to complain, for example, about a character appearing distasteful when in fact the quality of distastefulness is more important to Lindsay's scheme than the character himself. We are apt, like characters in *A Voyage to Arcturus,* to mistake the "flow for the ebb" (p. 72). If we attempt to apply traditional standards of novel criticism, borrowed again from the Victorians, to *A Voyage to Arcturus*, we will run aground even more quickly than we do with MacDonald's *Phantastes* or *Lilith.* Characterization shifts from the allegorical to the realistic and back again; moral assumptions change from one page to the next; plot is episodic and traditional (following the quest structure of symbolic fantasy), and seems at times even to approach epic dimensions. Yet the standards of the novel, as we have already seen in looking at the reviews, are inevitably applied to *A Voyage to Arcturus.* There is as yet no fully workable aesthetic of fantasy, although no book demonstrates the need for one better than *A Voyage to Arcturus.*

A Voyage to Arcturus invites, even demands, close interpretation. Whatever myth Lindsay has created is for him very largely a device for his philosophical aims; he may indeed be the first writer to discover the more purely intellectual rhetorical uses of symbolic fantasy, for unlike MacDonald (and unlike such later writers as Lewis and Tolkien), he does not assume any universal moral laws; his other world is as alien in values as it is in landscapes and characters. Lewis hints at this when he suggests that Lindsay "is the first writer to discover what 'other planets' are really good for in fiction."[19] Myth may well be irreducible, and on this level the story of *A Voyage to Arcturus* needs no clarification: the stripping away of layers of illusion is apparent even to readers who have no idea just what these veils are meant to be or what Lindsay regards as reality. But the book is enriched by the complex interweaving of allusion to familiar tradition (such as the Prometheus myth) with originality that characterizes Lindsay's myth, and this is what I propose to explore now.

The book opens rather feebly with a seance in the residence of the rich South American merchant Montague Faull. One immediately notices the unusual nomenclature that is to be a major feature of the work, with names drawn from no one source and for no one purpose, but intended rather to serve as guideposts for our reactions, serving almost the function of an artificial language, as does the nomenclature of William Blake's prophetic books. Prolands, for example, is the name of the residence; it of course suggests "prologue," and that is just the function of these early chapters. The medium who is to conduct the seance is named Backhouse, perhaps revealing Lindsay's contempt for spiritualists and to a limited extent setting up unconscious reactions in the reader toward this character. The name Montague Faull is even more suggestive; one can read the name as merely a pun on the adjective "foul," which might well apply to the merchant, or as a suggestion of the fall of man, from which eventual redemption may be brought about through pain.

Lindsay's method for coining names seems to be a highly arbitrary one, as suggested by a passage from his notebooks in which he explains his coinage of a term: " 'The *apercu*, which springs from the air, when brooded upon produces the *brood-apercu*.' "[20] While we are spared a creature named "Broodapercu" in *A Voyage to Arcturus*, the name is not unlike many that we will in fact encounter and that we can discuss properly only in terms of suggestion and connotation. Of the central characters in the book, for example, "Maskull" carries the suggestions of "mask," "skull," and "masculine"—all of which could reasonably be applied to this character at one point or another in the narrative. (One could carry this a step further by noting that the skull is the mask of the brain, which is in Schopenhauer's terms the regulator of the will, but it is more often than not pointless to attempt to find such precise symbolic equivalents for Lindsay's character and place names.) In any event, Maskull is conscious man, oriented toward appearances and incapable of achieving reality by anything short of death (just as death brings about union with nature in MacDonald's *Phantastes*). Conversely, "Nightspore" suggests the darker, inner aspect of man's personality that is the seed for a new being, and it is Nightspore who takes over the quest after Maskull's death. "Krag," the tutelary figure of the narrative, carries hints of the Promethean myth and is the first of many

19

names we will encounter that suggest bleakness and pain—Starkness, Sorgie (suggesting the German *Sorge*), Tormance, Alppain, even Arcturus. The name Arcturus itself is highly suggestive and rich in associations, reminding us of the unhappy king freed by Fable in Novalis' *Heinrich von Ofterdingen;* of the constellation associated with King Arthur in Tudor myth; even, perhaps, of the mythical celestial city of Arcturus after which the Babylonian city of Assur was supposedly patterned. Most important, probably, is the association of Arcturus with the north, which for Lindsay is the source of the "purer" races of man (as we shall see in *Devil's Tor*) and the land of fewest illusions: thus, Maskull's journey on Tormance takes him on a consistently northward course.

Besides introducing the reader to Lindsay's idiosyncratic, Blakeian nomenclature, the opening chapter also sets up muted themes that will emerge in full force once the story shifts to Tormance. " 'I dream with open eyes,' " explains the medium Backhouse, " 'and others see my dreams' " (p. 13). This remark in some sense capsulizes the manner in which Crystalman holds sway over his world of illusion and suggests as well the association of Backhouse with Crystalman. (Also, in *The Haunted Woman,* a character will come to suspect that she may be only a part of someone else's dream.) One of Lindsay's favorite metaphors in all his work, music, is introduced via Scriabin (whose mixed-media experiments probably would have appealed to Lindsay and who would himself have likely been delighted at the idea of Swaylone's Island, where the "music" alters reality itself) and *The Magic Flute,* which also suggests illusion and enchantment. Music will play an important role throughout the novel, from acting as an overall structural principle (the fugal manner in which Lindsay introduces and recapitulates themes), to serving as a plot device (the drum-taps that guide Maskull), to merely intensifying the emotional impact of a scene (the increasingly violent music that accompanies the vision induced by Dreamsinter), to providing the central metaphor of a particular value-system on Tormance (Earthrid's music of Swaylone's Island).

But the most significant theme in this opening chapter is perhaps the most subtle: the theme of illusion and pleasure (I regard this as a single theme because Lindsay often seems to regard them as virtually inseparable). The entire purpose for which the seance has been organized is entertainment and diversion, or pleasure, and each of the characters in this scene is, at least on a social level, involved as much in self-delusion as in reality. (This social aspect of illusion, of the inability of individuals to see beyond the scope of their own narrow universes, is treated in a more conventional manner in Lindsay's later novel, *The Haunted Woman.*) The specific social illusions involved in the opening chapter—Mrs. Jameson's immersion in art, Kent-Smith's concern with his own past and his autobiography, Faull's social dilettantism—do not seem to have specific parallels on Tormance, where such illusions are raised to the level of abstract principles governing all behavior, but they do serve as a useful, and accessible, prelude by introducing Lindsay's major themes in an ordinary and "realistic" social context.

Before the seance begins, Maskull and Nightspore enter. As soon as they are introduced to the company, a loud crash is heard—but only by those who happen to be in that part of the room in which the materialization is supposed to take place. Although we will later discover that this noise indeed does have a source (on Tormance), at the moment it only adds to the web of apparent illusion (I use the phrase "apparent illusion" advisedly, since we will later learn that what seems to be illusion in one order of existence may well turn out to be reality in another order). Similarly, Backhouse's intense physical strain in producing the materialization seems suspect initially, but we will encounter a similar kind of physical oppression when Maskull attempts to climb the tower at Starkness and when Nightspore, much later, tries to climb the tower of Muspel. Throughout this first chapter, Lindsay is preparing us for a reversal of expectations. The narrator is detached and objective, maintaining a distance from each character that allows us to regard these characters unsympathetically. Such devices as the highly artificial names and the almost gratuitously sketchy characterization aid in creating an overall air of artificiality. But when the narrative viewpoint finally centers on Maskull, we have little choice but to believe that what is unexplained is nonetheless a part of real experience and that it is, if anything, experience itself that is illusory. The apparent illusions or "supernatural" occurrences of life on Earth are the realities of Tormance; only the frame of reference is different. A similar reversal is effected with the character Krag, who is regarded as a villain or even a devil by many characters and whose initial appearance to the reader is equally repugnant, but who turns out to be the true agent of Muspel and the tutelary advocate of the hero.

The remaining chapters of the opening section of *A Voyage to Arcturus* describe the preparations of Maskull, Nightspore, and Krag to visit Tormance. Unexplained mystery is piled upon unexplained mystery: how do Maskull and Nightspore know each other, and how did Mrs. Trent come to invite them to the seance? What makes her suspect them to be mediums? How does Nightspore know Krag, and by what means did Krag arrive at the seance? Lindsay does not ignore such questions—most are asked openly at one time or another by the characters themselves—but he disdains them. " 'You are looking for mysteries,' " Krag explains to Maskull, " 'so naturally you are finding them' " (p. 25). As in MacDonald, we come to suspect that such passages as this in Lindsay are very largely addressed to the reader concerning the work itself. In the case of *A Voyage to Arcturus*, it is well that Lindsay should thus try to anticipate the reader's impatience. Surtur and Crystalman are mentioned in this same chapter, but the reader is given not the slightest explanation of who or what they might be. A mysterious lens with telescopic properties is produced by one of the characters. Maskull wonders, not unreasonably, if he is dreaming. He and Nightspore proceed a few days later to Starkness Observatory, the point of departure to Arcturus, and wait there for Krag. Nightspore introduces Maskull to the mysterious "drum-taps of Sorgie"

(p. 35), an eerie, rhythmic beating that can be heard on Earth only at the desolate Gap of Sorgie and suggests that Maskull may hear the sound again someday. Indeed, that sound is to be one of the unifying elements of the narrative. Maskull attemps to climb the tower of the observatory at Starkness and finds it painfully oppressive; he cannot complete the climb without the aid of Krag, who cuts Maskull's arm and spits on it. A voice warns Maskull against Nightspore, saying that Maskull will go, but Nightspore will return. Finally the night of departure arrives, and the three set off in a crystal torpedo propelled by "Arcturan back rays." The Introductory section of the story—among the weakest in terms of narrative power, but thematically among the most important—closes with Maskull falling asleep on the journey to Arcturus.

Two other important motives are introduced in these early chapters: the mysterious drum-taps and the image of crystal. The drum-taps I have already mentioned as a narrative device, but crystal is far more than that, calling to mind the "crystal self" that Raven speaks of in MacDonald's *Lilith* and especially the system of physiological evolution from crystal to spirit that Reil devised, influencing the German romantics and probably Schopenhauer as well. First, we encounter the hideous Crystalman grin on the face of the dead phantom during the seance; later the three central characters are whisked off in a crystal torpedo. We are also told that Tormance, their destination, is "Crystalman's country" (p. 24); thus a crystal torpedo seems an appropriate means of transportation there. Once on Tormance, we will encounter crystal plants, crystal eggs, and many similar images. Schopenhauer also was fascinated by crystal, and his account of it may shed some light on Lindsay's use of the image:

> ... the Idea that reveals itself in any general force of nature has always one single expression, although it presents itself differently according to the external relations that are present: otherwise its identity could not be proved, for this is done by abstracting the diversity that arises merely from external relations. In the same way the crystal has only *one* manifestation of life, crystallization, which afterwards has its fully adequate and exhaustive expression in the rigid form, the corpse of that momentary life.[21]

Throughout most of Maskull's experience on Tormance, the only reality we can be sure of is death (and perhaps pain); the Crystalman grin appears when the reality encounters the illusory world of Crystalman, like the final realization of some hideous cosmic joke. Schopenhauer's account of crystallization as a kind of "death," which in large part may in fact be drawn from Reil's earlier treatise, resembles Lindsay's notion. Schopenhauer further writes:

> In the forming of the crystal we see, as it were, a tendency towards an attempt at life, to which, however, it does not attain, because of the fluidity of which, like a living thing, it is composed at the moment of that movement is not enclosed in a *skin* ... and consequently it has neither vessels in which that movement could go on, nor does anything

separate it from the external world. Therefore, rigidity at once seizes that momentary movement, of which only the trace remains as the crystal.[22]

Crystal, then, suggests a striving at life that is thwarted by the process of crytallization. We will see a similar thwarting of movement toward life in Nightspore's final vision in the tower of Muspel. In these opening chapters, however, crystal is a more ambiguous image, and we do not realize, for example, the significance of the crystal torpedo or of the fact that it is guided by Krag, who we will later discover to be the greatest enemy of Crystalman.

There is little in the scene of Maskull's arrival on Tormance to suggest that this is a world caught up in the snares of illusion and pleasure. His first sensations are of intense weight and numbing pain, the latter of which will act "from now onward as a lower, sympathetic note to all his other sensations" (p. 45), although he may occasionally forget that it is there. Whatever the vague, quasi-science-fiction devices that Lindsay may use to get his protagonist into another world, it soom becomes clear that this new world is one of epic proportions and that the narrative has become elevated to an heroic level. We already know that Maskull is "a kind of giant, but of broader and more robust physique than most giants" (p. 18); throughout the rest of the novel he will be associated with Prometheus, from his intoduction to the visionary and poet Panawe, who associates Maskull with "a man in your world who stole something from the Maker of the universe, in order to ennoble his fellow creatures" (p. 61), to the character Dreamsinter, who tells Maskull, " 'You came to steal Muspel-fire, to give a deeper life to men—never doubting if your soul could endure the burning' " (p. 152). Adding to this heroic dimension of the narrative is the exaggerated, outsize world of Tormance (whose very name suggests both "torment" and the Italian *torma*, meaning crowd or swarm), with its oppressive gravity, savage landscapes that conform to the moral nature of each country they represent, and the massive double sun Arcturus, of which one twin, Branchspell, is alone "three times the apparent diameter" of our own sun (p. 51).

The dual suns play an important role in the narrative, representing the dual nature of Tormance—the familiar world of red, blue, and yellow primary colors opposed to the alien world of Alppain, the second sun, whose primary colors are "ulfire," "jale," and blue (p. 238). Since this color-scheme is to play an important symbolic role in the moral structure of Tormance, it might be worthwhile to discuss it briefly. When the new primary colors of ulfire and jale are first introduced, we are immediately given Maskull's sensory and psychological impressions of them:

Just as blue is delicate and mysterious, yellow clear and unsubtle, and red sanguine and passionate, so he felt ulfire to be wild and painful, and Jale dreamlike, feverish, and voluptuous (p.53).

Later, the character Corpang interprets the two sets of primary colors in terms of an ontological trinity of sorts, with each color given a fixed value:

23

Blue is existence. It is darkness seen through light; a contrasting of existence and nothingness. Yellow is relation. In yellow light we see the relation of objects in the clearest way. Red is feeling. When we see red, we are thrown back on our personal feelings. . . . As regards the Alppain colors, blue stands in the middle and is therefore not existence but relation. Ulfire is existence; so it must be a different sort of existence (p. 238).

Existence, then, "delicate and mysterious" in the familiar blue-oriented world of Branchspell, becomes "wild and painful" when translated into the different order of colors under Alppain. Furthermore, what appears as existence under Branchspell becomes merely relation under Alppain, suggesting that the color-order of Alppain is a step closer to reality, which is itself represented by Muspel-light, which casts no shadows (p. 221) and is wholly without color, resembling "nothing" (p. 259).

Van Mensing has suggested that Lindsay may have borrowed the idea of using different color systems to represent different orders of reality from Nietzsche, and indeed the passage Mensing cites from Nietzsche's *Beyond Good and Evil* is striking when regarded in terms of Lindsay's twin suns. Nietzsche writes:

As in the realm of stars an orbit of a planet is in some cases determined by two suns; as in certain cases suns of different colors shine near a single planet, sometimes with red light, sometimes with green light, and then occasionally illuminating the planet at the same time and flooding it with colors—so we modern men are determined, thanks to the complicated mechanics of our 'starry sky,' by *different* moralities; our actions shine alternately in different colors, they are rarely univocal—and there are cases enough in which we perform actions of *many colors.* [23]

Mensing suggests that the two suns of Tormance represent the different moralities of pleasure and pain, but if we look schematically at the two sets of primary colors in the novel, we can see that Alppain, which from its name would suggest the principle of pain, in fact contains its own pleasure principle in the color jale:

Color-Symbolism
in *A Voyage to Arcturus*

Principle:	feeling	relation	existence
Sun: Branchspell	red: "sanguine and passionate"	yellow: "clear and unsubtle"	blue: "delicate and mysterious"
Alppain	jale: "dreamlike, feverish, and voluptuous"	blue:	ulfire: "wild and painful"

24

The chart reveals that, while indeed there is no principle of pain represented in the colors of Branchspell (which are of course the same primary colors as our own world), the colors of Alppain oppose a pleasure principle (jale) and a pain principle (ulfire), with blue mediating between the two as "relation." Since blue in the more familiar order of things is regarded as existence, we might infer that this vision of existence is only a part, or branch, of the more fundamental reality represented by Alppain (hence, perhaps, "branch" versus "all" embedded in the names of the two suns). But this particular branch of reality exerts such a powerful spell over us (branch plus spell) that we cannot recognize the true nature of reality, which, as Nightspore will eventually discover, is pain (all plus pain).

Other color symbolism occurs from time to time in the novel; we are told the character Haunte, for example, has "dolm"-colored skin (p. 238), dolm being a compound of ulfire and blue, while the sensual Sullenbode has skin the color of jale and white (p. 242). White seems fairly consistently associated with pleasure and illusion, and green with life, especially in the scene of Nightspore's final vision from Muspel in Chapter 21.

Joiwind, the first character Maskull encounters on Tormance (Chapter 6), is dressed in pale green, suggesting life, but life only faintly realized. Her hair is flaxen, her skin pale and opalescent with many changing colors (none of which are vivid), her blood also milky and opalescent, and her diet simply water (which may account for some of the opalescence). She introduces Maskull to the first of many moral systems he is to encounter on Tormance, a system guided by the principles of self-sacrifice and "lovingkindness." " 'What pleasure is greater than lovingkindness?' " she asks ingenuously (p. 48), but we will soon learn that the word "pleasure" is a signal of the presence of Crystalman and his illusions. When Joiwind mixes her blood with Maskull's to give him the strength to travel in the fierce gravity of Tormance, he feels a "stream of pleasure" enter his veins. Joiwind claims that Surtur, whom Maskull says he has come in pursuit of, is also known as Shaping and Crystalman. She also explains to him the uses of three new organs he has sprouted—the "breve," for telepathy; the "poigns" (perhaps from "poignant"), for sympathy with life; and the "magn," for deeper love (though when Joiwind kisses Maskull with her magn, the kiss is sexless). The paleness and insubstantiality of Joiwind reflect the moral system of her region, called "Poolingdred." At first this system seems attractive, but Lindsay believes otherwise. Van Mensing again invokes Nietzsche, who writes: " 'Refraining mutually from injury, violence, and exploitation and placing one's will on a part with that of someone else . . . immediately proves to be what it really is—a will to the *denial* of life, a principle of disintegration and decay.' "[24]

Panawe, Joiwind's equally pale husband, is the principle spokesman for this part of the book (Chapter 7) and introduces the intellectual themes of the story that have earlier been confined to imagery and cryptic remarks. His semi-shamanistic wisdom and insight causes him to associate Maskull with Prometheus, and he speaks with apparent true wisdom and authority. He is, in fact, the spokesman for the moral world of Poolingdred, just as Joiwind is the image of its ideal. The three of them walk on water—another image of insubstantial being, although one with obvious Christian overtones—and Panawe coughs up a pale green crystal, which prompts Maskull to label him an artist, one who puts forth beautiful things. But Panawe says, " 'Nothing comes of it but vanity' " (p. 63). The myriad, crystal-based life forms that they encounter near Poolingdred are explained by Panawe in terms of the fluidity of nature. " 'The will forks and sports incessantly,' " he comments of the young world of Tormance, and later adds that this sporting is the " 'blind will to become like Shaping' " (p. 65). ("Will" is another word that we will pick up as an indication of the influence of Crystalman.) This whole region is keyed to the principle of self-sacrifice—even a plant cries to a flying worm seeking nectar," 'To me! To me' " (p. 65)! But we are given some indications that this is not all there is to Tormance: Maskull once again hears the mysterious drumbeats that he first heard at the Gap of Sorgie, and catches sight of the battlement-like mountains of the violent land of Ifdawn Marest. He also sees the blue light of the second sun, Alppain, although the sun itself cannot be seen from Poolingdred.

At home Panawe tells Maskull some incidents of his life, starting with his bisexual birth. This introduces yet another important theme—that of ambiguous sexual identity—that is to persist as one of the unresolved images of dualism throughout the book. Each individual contains a struggle of male and female forces; one can win out only at the cost of the death of the other. Life is realized only by death (just as, in Schopenhauer, pleasure is realized only by pain). In Panawe, these forces were balanced, but the female part of him sacrificed herself to the male (throughout the book, sacrifice is presented as a female principle). This account of individuation, oriented as it is to Lindsay's overall theme of will, bears remarkable similarity to Jungian theory, in which aspects of the archetypal mother and father figures must be overcome for the individual consciousness to achieve identity. But willing sacrifice is not ordinarily a part of this process. Other incidents related by Panawe involve his encounter and brief debate with the sorcerer Slofork on a narrow ridge, which ends in Slofork's suicide; and his meeting in Ifdawn Marest with the villain Muremaker, who hangs suspended over an abyss by the will of another and who will fall into the abyss when that will fails. After Panawe's narrative, the three characters sleep, and Maskull, on awaking, feels drawn to Ifdawn Marest. He takes leave of his companions and sets off to the north, which will continue to be his principal direction of travel throughout the remainder of the narrative.

I have dwelt at some length upon this initial episode of Maskull's adventures on Tormance to demonstrate how Lindsay begins to construct his rhetorical meanings apart from, and in this case in opposition to, the conventional narrative or novelistic expectations of the reader. Joiwind and Panawe are certainly sympathetic characters, and Lindsay does not condemn them specifically anywhere in the book. But of all the images, symbols, and narrative devices that are introduced in this section, only a few will remain constant throughout the narrative. It is up to the reader to pick up these constants and realize that they are collectively the symbolic axis of the entire fantasy and that all other images must be interpreted in relation to them. Crystal, for example, is oppressive to life and rich in illusion; in Nightspore's final vision from Muspel, the imprisoned green spark of life in crystal "was so minute as to be scarcely visible" (p.283). Crystalman is the antagonist, the master of illusion who thwarts all life as it strives toward Muspel. Yet Joiwind claims that "Crystalman" is merely a term of endearment for Surtur—who is in reality the guardian of Muspel and Crystalman's worst enemy. Most of the vegetation in Poolingdred is of crystal—perhaps frozen into that form as it moved toward sentient life. Alppain, whose light is the color of intellect or "true relation," is not visible from Poolingdred. We begin to suspect, perhaps, that this world, even with its noble principles of self-sacrifice and "lovingkindness," is grounded in illusion. But this suspicion does not fully emerge until long after Maskull has left this region.

Furthering this suspicion is the account of Panawe's past experiences. Joiwind comments earlier that Panawe had once met a man who " 'believed the universe to be, from top to bottom, a conjuror's cave' " (p. 57). The reader does not know it yet, but this view represents Lindsay's own concept of the world, especially of the world of Tormance, yet neither Joiwind nor Panawe are willing to accept it. The sorcerer Slofork may well be this man. Panawe responds well to most of his questions, but he cannot go beyond the accepted values of pleasure, pain, and love. Slofork does go beyond these values. There is a world of deeper experience, he suggests, " 'and there all this is unknown, and another order of things reigns. That world we call Nothing—but it is not Nothing, but Something' " (p. 72). Panawe apparently does not comprehend; he makes a "sententious" statement about wisdom being misery, to which the sorcerer replies, " 'You will never rise above mysticism,' " and plunges into the void. Later, Panawe is terrified by his encounter with the effects of will in the person of Muremaker, but he fails to see that will is a part of his own life, that the principles he lives by derive from will and that, in fact, Muremaker's imminent plunge into the abyss rather parallels Slofork's plunge, the central difference being that Slofork's own will controlled his fate.

Lindsay cannot wholly condemn sacrifice, for it is sacrifice of a much higher order that permits Maskull to be transformed. But sacrifice in relation to others is an illusion of the will. Panawe and Joiwind are victims of this illusion, though not perpetrators of it; they are in fact in a state resembling primal innocence in their cup-like mountain, and as such they provide an appropriate introduction to this new world. Rhetorically, however, this may prove confusing to the reader: we are already following the viewpoint of the conventionally ingenuous narrator of symbolic fantasy; to have him introduced to his new world by characters who are themselves ingenuous as to its true nature risks losing the reader altogether. Yet this device is necessary to make the education, or process of discovery, of

Maskull rhetorically effective. If innocence is not presented at the outset in this particular narrative, it will not seem at all convincing, and the innocence here is a genuine kind of innocence, and not a deliberate pretense. Also, the structure of the fantasy demands that each succeeding section encompass the values of the preceeding while seeming to deny them. Self-sacrifice is thus presented as at once the simplest and most universal of illusions, appearing in the noblest of guises.

As Maskull leaves Poolingdred, Panawe sings a song which, like Krag's earlier comment concerning mysteries, and like the fairies' song taunting Anodos in MacDonald's *Phantastes*, is presented as a thinly veiled message to the reader. The song

> seemed to be always just on the point of becoming clear and intelligible—not with the intelligibility of words, but in the way one sympathizes with another's moods and feelings, and Maskull felt that something important was about to be uttered, which would explain all that had gone before. But it was invariably postponed, he never understood—and yet somehow he did understand (p. 76).

Such devices may seem awkward and gratuitous, but they do serve to prepare the reader for the "unknowable" nature of Lindsay's final position.

The second moral realm Maskull enters, (Chapter 8) corresponding roughly with his second day on Tormance, is that of duty. An interlude with a being claiming to be Surtur on the Lusion Plain convinces Maskull that he exists only to serve this supreme being, that he is "a man of destiny" (p. 79). He enters Ifdawn Marest, a region of life as violent as Poolingdred was subdued; even the name suggests hazards ("if dawn"). Here he encounters a beautiful if masculine woman named Oceaxe, with whose aid he changes his telepathic organ of will and his love-tentacle for a grasping third arm. Organs of sharing are replaced by organs of control, and the feeling Maskull experiences during the process is one of "healing pain" (p. 83). Pain, it must be remembered, is a thematic constant, always bringing Maskull nearer to reality. His new organs will be necessary in the violent world of Ifdawn, and he soon learns to use them in a victorious contest of wills with Oceaxe's lover Crimtyphon (whose name, Mensing suggests, combines "crime," "Christ," and "Typhon" of Greek mythology [25]).

Both for the sake of dramatic contrast and to further reveal his philosophical system, Lindsay moves the reader from a world in which will is subordinated to a "higher" principle into a world in which will is an essential prerequisite for survival. Since the world of Ifdawn openly recognizes the force of will, it exists on a higher plane (both literally and figuratively) than Poolingdred; but its characters, by openly acknowledging the power of will, at first appear less noble than Panawe or Joiwind. However, they are certainly more *real*: Oceaxe is the first truly sexual being Maskull encounters on Tormance, and it is apparent from the manner in which Lindsay treats her and other characters that he places value on the passionate, dangerous life of Ifdawn Marest, subject as this life is to the will. No believer in the principle of "saving illusions," Lindsay seems to find passion a step closer to reality than altruism. Love, as experienced through Maskull's new arm, is a kind of fierce sexual longing (p. 94); the landscapes produce not aesthetic sensations, but a strong desire for some kind of immediate action. Life is to be acted upon, and not merely passively experienced, in the way Panawe and Joiwind experienced it. Even the landscape reflects this need for quick action: it rises and falls without warning; beasts are mentally controlled by force of will—the entire region is an imaginative projection of the negative aspect of the will.

Maskull kills Crimtyphon in the same way Krag killed the apparition at the seance—by twisting his neck completely around. The Crystalman grin appears for the first time on Tormance. But Oceaxe contends that this hideous smile appears on the face of everyone who dies (p. 105), indicating the extent of control that Crystalman exercises over Tormance. She, too, believes Crystalman and Surtur to be one. Maskull again sees the light of Alppain, but here its effect is different from what it was in Poolingdred. Whereas there it had caused torment and "restless and noble" feelings, here it brings on "a peculiar wave of self-denial" (p. 106), suggesting that this sun represents not an absolute value, but rather an abstract quality that might best be described as *otherness*—as the moral alternative to whatever region Maskull is in at the moment, just as the colors of Alppain suggest otherness and the principle of relative existence. In this manner, the sun also serves to a limited extent to foreshadow each succeeding episode, which (on the surface at least) represents a reversal of the values of the previous one.

There follows a curious episode in which Tydomin, Crimtyphon's other and older lover, appears and kills Oceaxe by means of thought-control. She then claims that the light of Alppain means sacrifice and rightly prophesies that Maskull's adventures on Tormance must ultimately end in sacrifice. This is not the loving, pleasurable self-sacrifice of Joiwind—it is rather " 'a penalty which we pay' " (p. 113). What Tydomin is leading up to is simply that she wants to occupy Maskull's body. This is the sacrifice that she demands of him, and what it amounts to is a complete submission to her will. Maskull does not fully understand such hunger of the will until he "absorbs" Joiwind's brother Digrung later in the narrative. (Digrung dies without the Crystalman grin, but this may be because he is not really dead; later, as Maskull approaches Digrung's home country of Matterplay, he begins to feel stirrings, presumably of the absorbed Digrung, inside himself.) Maskull and Tydomin enter her cave moments before an avalanche crashes past the entrance; this is the crashing noise heard during the seance in the first chapter (pp. 18, 122). Maskull submits to Tydomin and soon finds himself back in the room of the seance on Earth, only this time he is himself the apparition. Krag enters and breaks his neck, and he awakes again in Tydomin's cave, only now with the knowledge that she must die. Maskull's "murder" on Earth serves the purpose of effecting his release from the enchantment of Tydomin on Tormance.

This is the only point in the narrative at which Krag actively intervenes to save Maskull from illusion. Maskull comes to realize that this is a false sacrifice to Tydomin, a mere submission to her destructive will. This symbolic death and rebirth of the hero represents the first stripping away of illusions—in this case, the illusions of the value of sacrifice and the beneficent will. Just how far Maskull has become entangled in this world of illusion is apparent when he views his former self on Earth, from the vantage point of the apparition at the seance. It is "as if a crime-riddled man of middle age were suddenly confronted with his own photograph as an earnest, idealistic youth" (p. 123). From this point on, Maskull will find it easier to see through the false values of the various regions of Tormance as he gradually comes to realize his true mission. As narrative, however, the time scheme of the episode does not quite work out, since the seance occurred before Maskull left for Tormance and he thus apparently has to travel back in time to reappear at it (although a number of explanations of this apparent inconsistency offer themselves: first, it may be merely a vision induced by Krag. Or, more complexly, we might guess that Maskull actually does return to Earth. Since we are told earlier that it takes light a hundred years to reach Earth from Arcturus but that the journey in the crytal torpedo takes only nineteen hours (p. 29), we can surmise that Maskull in fact travels into the past in going to Arcturus—nearly a century into the past, since the light from that star will not arrive on earth for a hundred years. But then one is faced with the problem of how Maskull does in fact return: if he travels at the speed of light, the trip would take a century; but if he travels at the speed of the crystal torpedo, he would arrive years before the seance takes place. What seems most likely is that Lindsay himself never really bothered to work the situation out logically.)

Tydomin, it seems, represents a step further in the direction of pure will than did Oceaxe. She is presented as being rather cold and unsympathetic, whereas the earlier woman was passionate and fierce; hence Tydomin is the greater threat to Maskull and must be destroyed. Again we can invoke Erich Neumann's interpretation of the hero myth, in which the emerging hero must overcome two incestuous aspects of the Great Mother —the uroboric, which threatens to absorb the germinal ego back into the unconscious; and the matriarchal, which involves seduction by the mother and final castration.[26]

Maskull condemns Tydomin to death, but first she must lead him to Sant, a curious, womanless country on a high plateau (Chapter 12). They encounter Spadevil, a resident of Sant (perhaps from French sante, "health") who changes their sorbs to "probes," or organs of duty (p. 133). Spadevil is a spectacular character, who first appears walking fearlessly amid lightning, appearing more distinct than the natural world around him, his flesh the color of iron. His name contains many associations: spade, appropriate to one whose organs are called probes and whose flesh is the color of iron; spado, an archaic term for eunuch—appropriate to his sexlessness and hatred of women; spaeman, a Scottish term for a prophet or wizard; and of course devil and evil. He tells the travelers that through brooding and rejection, he has arrived at the new law of duty. He is the

30

prophet of a legendary figure called Hator, and Maskull and Tydomin are to be his first disciples. Hator had taught that a world based on pleasure is inferior to a world based on grandeur, but Maskull replies that " 'The individual spirit that lives and wishes to live is mean and corrupt-natured' " (p. 137). Spadevil rejects this argument. Although he truly believes that the illusions of pleasure are dangerous, he cannot realize, as Maskull eventually does, that duty is " 'but a cloak under which we share the pleasure of other people' " (p. 145). As Mensing points out, Spadevil is one of Nietzsche's " 'preachers of repentance' " who " 'talk of "duties," and actually always of duties that are supposed to be unconditional.' "[27]

Even higher than Ifdawn Marest, Sant is the most elevated moral region of all those that Maskull has visited so far on the planet Tormance. The law of Sant, established by the ancient prophet Hator and symbolized by Hator's Trifork, is hatred of pleasure and dependence upon pain as a moral principle. Spadevil himself show this to be false, insofar as for the residents of Sant, hatred of pleasure " 'is the greatest pleasure to them' " (p. 135). Sant is, literally, a black-and-white world (p. 141), and this is reflected in its simplistic values. The false asceticism of Sant, like the false duty of Spadevil, becomes apparent to Maskull when he finally rejects both value-systems (p. 145), but many of the insights he gains in this episode are true. When Spadevil dies, we do not know whether or not he wears the Crystalman grin (p. 147), even though the body of Tydomin, who has also accepted his teaching, does. Perhaps Lindsay is suggesting that duty is an acceptable moral principle for Spadevil himself, but that his illusion is in believing it to be a general moral system which he must evangelize upon to others. Spadevil is in fact presented in evangelical Christian terms when he speaks of bearing the new law (p. 132) and being prepared to lay down his life (p.139; cf. John 10:15-18), but it would be premature to suggest that he represents Lindsay's final view of Christianity. That will come later.

The religion of Sant, with its legends of Hator, its high priest Catice, and its strict moral laws, is the most complex system of belief that Lindsay establishes on Tormance with the possible exception of Threal. It serves the important function of revealing to us that Surtur and Shaping are *not* the same (p. 145), despite what Joiwind and Oceaxe believed; that pleasure is at least one major enemy to be dealt with; and that pain may be an effective means of dealing with it, as long as pain does not become an end in itself, as it does in Sant. When Maskull awakes the next morning to his third day on Tormance, the second stage of his education is complete. Just as a realization of the false nature of sacrifice stripped away his illusions regarding himself in relation to others, so a realization of the false nature of duty destroys his illusions regarding himself in relation to any abstract moral order. He awakes to the knowledge that throughout the previous day he had been "under a series of heavy enchantments" (p. 150) by Oceaxe, Tydomin, Spadevil, and finally Catice.

Maskull finds himself in the Wombflash Forest (Chapter 13), and he hears once again the drumbeats, only now, for the first time, he intuitively associates them with Surtur—another indication of his moral progress. He meets Dreamsinter, who is perhaps an agent of Surtur, since he seems to be strangling in the atmosphere of Tormance (which is, after all, an atmosphere of illusion and deceit). Dreamsinter feeds Maskull a bitter fruit that induces a symbolic vision of his future fate: death at the hands of Krag, followed by Nightspore continuing the quest toward Muspel-light. Self-realization continues to dawn on Maskull, and Dreamsinter tells him for the first time what his real mission on Tormance is: to steal Muspel fire to ennoble his fellow man (p. 152). The interlude is brief, like the earlier encounter with Surtur-Shaping on the Lusion Plain, and it serves largely as a transition into Maskull's third day of adventures.

Until now, the larger issues Lindsay has dealt with—the relation of the individual to others, principles of self-determination, moral laws—could easily have been dealt with effectively in a less unusual form than that of the symbolic fantasy. But now, following a series of almost Cartesian reductions, Lindsay proceeds to deal with the nature of the individual in relation to nature itself, or to perceived reality. After making his way out of the forest (Chapter 14) and taking a brief swim, Maskull arrives at a slightly different view of himself from any he has heretofore held:

> He was a naked stranger in a huge, foreign, mystical world, and which-ever way he turned, unknown and threatening forces were glaring at him. The gigantic, white, withering Branchspell, the awful, body-changing Alppain, the beautiful, deadly, treacherous sea, the dark and eerie Swaylone's Island, the spirit-crushing forest out of which he had just escaped—to all these mighty powers, surrounding him on every side, what resources had he . . . (p. 159).

The natural world, which had previously existed largely only in terms of the moral laws of its inhabitants (such as the treacherous terrain of Ifdawn Marest reflecting the treachery of its inhabitants), here appears as a force-ful, passive kind of grandeur, seeming to represent in some respect a giant moral force divorced from will, and a force that must eventually be con-fronted by any discoverer of reality.

The first character Maskull encounters in this natural world is, appro-priately, Polecrab the fisherman. Polecrab is an image of natural man in balance with his environment; he does not set up metaphysical problems nor does he purport to answer them. What answers he does offer Maskull involve the lay of the land to the north—Maskull's perennial direction of travel—and simple facts about his own land and Swaylone's Island, which is visible some distance from the shore. Polecrab has received wisdom from Broodviol, the wise man that Panawe told Maskull about earlier, but he can make little of it, and is not even sure if he remembers it correctly (p. 166). He has true wisdom, though he denies it, but it is wisdom of a lower order, of the common sense, unimaginative man who can exist with nature because he never questions nature and who can never actively par-take of an heroic quest like Maskull's. When Maskull speaks of him as "a mountain wrapped in a cloud" (p. 175), he speaks more of potential than of reality.

Gleameil, Polecrab's wife, has a different attitude toward nature, and is a foreshadowing of the visionary women characters who so powerfully will come to dominate Lindsay's later fiction. Like Eve, she is curious, and the object of her curiosity is Earthrid's "painful" music, capable of conjuring "the most astonishing forms, which are not phantasms, but reality" (p. 168), and which comes from Swaylone's Island. Such music again calls to mind Nietzsche: "'The truly Dionysian music presents itself as such a general mirror of the universal will; the vivid event refracted in this mirror expands at once for our consciousness to the copy of an external truth.'"[28] Gleameil is like Maskull, in that she claims to be "'conscious of two worlds. My husband and boys are real to me, and I love them fondly. But there is another world for me, as there is for you, Maskull, and it makes my real world appear all false and vulgar.'" (Chapter 15, p. 175). Abandoning her family, Gleameil sets out with Maskull for Swaylone's Island.

They arrive at the island and interrogate Earthrid the musician, whose account of reality in terms of music reflect's Lindsay's own increasing notion that music alone can approach the pure expression of the sublime. Earthrid agrees to play when the moon called Teargeld rises. Just as Alppain and Branchspell represent two orders of existence—the familiar and the alien—so Teargeld reflects the rays of both and, like a work of art (like A Voyage to Arcturus itself, in fact), represents a bringing together of the two worlds. Earthrid plays his "music," and it alters nature to conform to its own passion and pain, perhaps the pain that leads to reality. This is too much for Gleameil, who dies with the Crystalman grin on her face, having discovered pain where she had expected beauty (p. 183). Maskull survives, however, and insists on trying to play the instrument (a lake named Irontick) himself, and despite Earthrid's objections and warnings he does so, attempting to portray on it, through his will, a reality that corresponds to the Muspel-light he sees (p. 185). The result is catastrophic: both Irontick and Earthrid are destroyed (Earthrid possibly without the Crystalman grin), and Maskull is again alone. No reality created by man—no art—can really correspond to Muspel.

Maskull next enters Matterplay (Chapter 16), a land of great fertility, indicating that he is getting nearer to the source of life. (His means of getting to Matterplay is a stream of moving water reminiscent of Anodos's river that takes him to the fairy palace in MacDonald's Phantastes.) Stirrings within him suggest that Digrung is trying to assert himself (p. 189), and Maskull almost succumbs to the temptation to see things through Digrung's consciousness. He finally does sprout Digrung's eyes, and through them he catches a glimpse of the origin of life:

The green sparks from the brook, when closely watched, could be distinguished individually, each one wavering up toward the clouds, but the moment they got within them a fearful struggle seemed to begin. The spark endeavored to escape through to the upper air, while the clouds concentrated around it, whichever way it darted, trying to create so dense a prison that further movement would be impossible (p. 196).

This is a foreshadowing of the vision Nightspore will have from the tower of Muspel. Maskull theorizes that this process is like the birth of thought, but he does not know yet who the thinker is.

He meets a strange, ancient being of a third sex, called a "phaen," who has spent his (or "aer," to use Lindsay's own coined pronoun) life searching for the god Faceny, who resides in the underground kingdom of Threal (which was also the home of Earthrid). The phaen, Leehallfae, leads Maskull along the stream of life and explains that Faceny "is all face" and faces nothingness in all directions (p. 203)—anticipating Nightspore's confrontation with nothingness from the tower of Muspel. Leehallfae again brings us closer to reality, but also suffers from illusion—in this case, the belief that Faceny exists as a surrogate to confront the nothingness that all beings must eventually confront as individuals. By an unlikely accident, Maskull and Leehallfae find the entrance to Threal and enter the enormous cavern. Here Leehallfae dies, the Crystalman grin on his face, and disappears into the nothingness from which he ("aer") came.

A new character, Corpang, appears (Chapter 17) and explains that such creatures of Faceny as Leehallfae cannot survive in Threal, which is the realm of another god, Thire. The trinity of existence, Corpang explains, consists of existence, relation, and passion, as expressed in the two primary color systems and the gods Faceny (face), Amfuse (perhaps, as Mensing suggests, from "fuse" or relation[29]), and Thire (presumably feeling). There is of course a suggestion of the Christian trinity (in which one might equate Father, Son, and Holy Ghost with existence, relation, and feeling), and like a Christian, Corpang worships the creator of life. But later, when Corpang accompanies Maskull and the two of them come upon idols representing the trinity of gods of Threal, Muspel-light changes each idol's face into a Crystalman mask. It is interesting to note that, although his quest is not yet complete, Maskull has already apparently begun his Promethean mission of bringing "deeper life to men" with Muspel-fire. Corpang is the only being on Tormance except Maskull to undergo the process of disillusionment and survive.

Maskull continues to the north with Corpang, but the relationship is now reversed: Maskull is the leader, the educator, and Corpang the student. Maskull is now hot on the trail of reality (so to speak), and only the greatest efforts of Crystalman are left to be brought against him. The two are greeted by Haunte, an aerial boatman from Lichstorm, a country of apparently pure sexuality and sexual segregation. Haunte offers to introduce Maskull to Sullenbode. Pure sexual passion is something Maskull has not yet encountered on Tormance—the closest he has come to it has been with Oceaxe, and with her it was but an instrument of sacrifice and the will to power—and it is of some importance that Lindsay places it this high in his scale of temptations. However, it seems appropriate that after rejecting all the disguised permutations of the will to live, Maskull should encounter it in its purest and most powerful form. Again we may invoke Schopenhauer, who also regarded sexuality as the physical basis of will; of sexual desire he writes:

It is everywhere tacitly assumed as necessary and inevitable, and is not, like other desires, a matter of taste and disposition. For it is the desire which even constitutes the nature of man. In conflict with it no motive is so strong that it would be certain of victory....it is really the invisible central point of all action and conduct....[30]

Thus what might seem the most obvious and easily overcome illusion is in a sense not illusion at all, but the reality which, at the center of consciousness, is the origin of destructive will and the chief quality in Maskull's character that could prevent him from ever achieving the heroic goal of Muspel. Notice how Lindsay describes his purely sexual creature, Sullenbode:

He thought he had never seen anything half so feminine. Her flesh was almost melting in its softness. So undeveloped were the facial organs that they looked scarcely human; only the lips were full, pouting, and expressive. In their richness, these lips seemed like a splash of vivid will on a background of slumbering protoplasm...(p. 242).

It seems likely that Lindsay here uses the lips as a euphemistic image for the sexual organs and that these lips contain the awful energy of pure will, energy powerful enough to destroy Haunte when, after having kissed her once, he attempts it a second time. Maskull, however, is capable of kissing her and bringing her from her unformed sexual state into being. Maskull's sexual ability derives solely from his heroic stature, from his slightly feminine characteristics (Haunte regarded himself as more purely masculine than Maskull, and therefore more completely opposed in nature to Sullenbode), from his strength of character developed by his adventures and augmented by the absorption of Digrung's personality, or from a combination of all these factors; at any rate, he has transformed Sullenbode into a tangible love object (even though her lips retain their strange fire), and she returns his love. Why Corpang seems unaffected by Sullenbode is also unclear.

Corpang, Sullenbode, and Maskull set off together for Adage, the highest peak of Lichstorm (where mountains are formed by the passions of rocks for other rocks), and Maskull recounts his experiences to Sullenbode, who observes that, in all his adventures, the women had been the most noble beings because of their principle of sacrifice (p. 252). Corpang, finding Sullenbode disagreeable for some reason, departs from them and goes off on his own. Just as he was the only Arcturan to survive disillusionment, so is he the only one to undertake his own quest for Muspel. Maskull and Sullenbode cross the Mornstab Pass and encounter full Muspel-light, which affects Maskull strongly but which is invisible to Sullenbode. When Sullenbode realizes that this light, invisible as it is, holds a greater attraction for Maskull than she does, she dies. Her face bears the Crystalman grin, indicating perhaps that Crystalman is the master of the source of will itself, but Maskull, in his grief over her death (and this is the only death in the entire narrative that he really seems to express grief over), does not see this. The final sacrifice that Tydomin had warned Maskull he must make is accomplished, it would at first seem. Although Maskull might have succumbed to the temptations of Sullenbode (and this is strongly evidenced by his reaction to her death), the attraction of Muspel-light proves finally stronger in him; he has in effect overcome the source of will and denied his own humanity. But the emotional emptiness he now feels gives him one more weakness, one more good chance for Crystal-man to delude him.

Alone again, Maskull descends into Barey, the last land before Muspel and the only land besides Muspel for which Lindsay draws the name from Eddic lore (Barey is referred to as "the frondiferous isle" in the *Younger Edda*[31]). He meets and recounts his experiences to Krag, who responds, " 'You think you are thoroughly disillusioned, don't you? Well, that may prove to be the last and strongest illusion of all' " (p. 265). Krag and Maskull pass through Barey, whose trees are asleep and waiting for the rising of Alppain, and they encounter Gangnet (a name perhaps drawn from the Eddic name of "Gangleri" for Wotan), a lazy but congenial character who tries through various devices, including invoking the memory of Sullenbode (p. 268), to convince Maskull that the world is not really a bad place after all and that his difficulties have arisen from the opposing wills of the two suns; all he has to do is choose one and renounce the other. But Krag scorns even renunciation (p. 269). Nevertheless, when Alppain finally rises, Gangnet convinces Maskull that his goal is nothingness, the annihilation of the will to achieve nonbeing, and Maskull accepts this: it is as far as he can go in Crystalman's world. Krag tells him he is dying, however, and in Maskull's final moments of life he realizes that Gangnet is Crystalman himself, and that Krag is the source of the drumbeats he has been following throughout the book. Nonbeing is as close as Maskull, the mask, the conscious man, can approach reality; his only true encounter with it is death, and we find that death has been his goal throughout the book. Nonbeing in the existential sense is the final illusion of Crystalman; only through death can the world of illusion be left behind. (This is really not too far removed from the kind of Christian Platonism in MacDonald that made the deaths of Anodos and Vane necessary elements in the moral structures of *Phantastes* and *Lilith*.) Thus, to give us his true vision of reality, Lindsay must eliminate Maskull, lest we think that Muspel, too, is but a mask, an illusion. As Krag later says of Crystalman, " 'Maskull was his, but Nightspore is mine' " (p. 277).

Here Lindsay departs slightly from the philosophical system of Schopenhauer that he has been following for much of the narrative, and approaches nearer to the kind of system we have already discussed in terms of *The Cloud of Unknowing* (although I do not mean to suggest that that book is the source of Lindsay's vision at this point). Nonbeing is not the goal in *Arcturus*, but only a means of reaching that goal, which is, like the Buddhist Nirvana, a higher reality. Lindsay wrote in his notebooks, " 'Schopenhauer's "Nothing," which is the least understood part of his system, is identical with my Muspel; that is the *real* world.' "[32] Simple nonbeing is only Crystalman's version of the Platonic reality represented by this larger Nothing.

For a metaphor of the real world, Lindsay turns to the *Younger Edda*. Again in his notes, he writes, " 'In the Norse mythology, Muspel is the primeval world of fire; existing before heaven and earth, and which will eventually destroy them.' "[33] The passage itself, in the *Younger Edda* of Snorri Sturleson, is as follows:

> ...there was in the southern region the world called Muspell. It is a world too luminous and glowing to be entered by those who are not indigenous there. He who sitteth on its borders (or the land's-end) to guard it is named Surtur. In his hand, he beareth a flaming falchion, and at the end of the world shall issue forth to combat, and shall vanquish all the gods, and consume the universe with fire.[34]

According to Fin Magnusen, Surtur was "the invisible, unintelligible being whom the ancient Scandinavians regarded as 'the great First Cause least understood' of all things."[35] He certainly serves something of the same function for Lindsay, even though he is finally revealed to be Krag—who in turn is revealed to be pain. In the final scenes of *A Voyage to Arcturus*, Nightspore, who can travel where Maskull could not, enters Muspel and climbs a tower similar to the one Maskull tried to climb at the Starkness Observatory on Earth; again the task grows increasingly laborious as he climbs the stairs, but unlike Maskull, Nightspore makes it to the top on his own—another indication that he has passed into a purer state.

There are six windows in the tower. The first two reveal nothing, but at the third, Nightspore sees a vision of a world made up of green crystals producing a marching rhythm and struggling against more powerful white shapes that produce a waltzing rhythm; the vision recalls Maskull's encounter with the stream of life in Matterplay and is clearly intended to be read as the principle of pleasure (represented by the waltzing rhythm) overcoming the more severe and rigorous principle of reality (represented by the martial rhythm). At the fourth window, this vision becomes clarified as the green corpuscles are revealed to be individual beings caught up in a "ghastly mush of soft pleasure" produced by the white forms. The fifth window shows how the dual forces came about: Crystalman acts as a prism to the life-force, or passion, emanating from Muspel, separating it into forward rays (white) moving away from Muspel or wishing to remain stationary, and back rays (green) striving to return to Muspel; we recall the Arcturan back rays that propelled the crystal torpedo. The final window reveals Crystalman as a shadowy being who feeds on the Muspel-stream for his own pleasure, resulting in the separation of life from will and making the two antagonistic, with the will the more powerful. Nightspore continues to the roof of the tower, hoping to find in Muspel the true answer to Crystalman. At first, he sees nothing, perceiving only a horribly "grinning" darkness, but then he realizes that Muspel is himself and the tower and that the tower is in danger of its very existence. Everything else belongs to Crystalman. Nightspore returns to Krag, who is known on earth as pain, and the two set off into the darkness. The narrative ends with a hint that the entire process may begin again on earth.

What is Muspel? It is no more a reducible symbol for Lindsay than Moby-Dick is for Melville—the inscrutable reality that lies behind all masks. But there is no way to discuss the brilliant, complex vision with which *A Voyage to Arcturus* ends without seeming reductive, and to attempt a broader discussion of Lindsay as philosopher on the basis of it alone would be premature. What is of great importance in terms of symbolic fantasy is that fantasy seems a necessary condition for the embodiment of this vision. Even had Lindsay chosen to write a purely expository tract and abandoned fiction altogether, he would have found it necessary to turn to fantasy for his metaphors and illustrations. Lindsay may have aspired to being a philosopher, and it is certainly true that his reputation will rest on the strength of his poetic vision rather than his skill at expressing it, but in any event, he succeeded in creating an effective heroic myth and in giving this myth a rhetorical base that derived from something outside the irreduceable structure of the story itself; and in this manner he broadened the possibilities of symbolic fantasy, and indeed of all philosophical fiction in the twentieth century.

Notes

1. Quoted in J. B. Pick, "A Sketch of Lindsay's Life as Man and Writer," in *The Strange Genius of David Lindsay* (London: John Baker, 1970), p. 3.
2. *Times Literary Supplement*, 5 July 1963, p. 497.
3. *"A Voyage to Arcturus,"* *Book Review Digest*, 60 (1964), p. 738.
4. "Adventures on a Distant Star," *New York Times Book Review*, 24 November 1963, p. 60.
5. "Science Fiction," *New York Review of Books*, 12 December 1963, pp. 23–24.
6. "The Arcturan Shadow," *Notes and Queries* [British], 30 March 1940, pp. 225–27.
7. "Arcturus and Christian Dogma," in Wilson, et al., *Strange Genius*.
8. "Sublimities in a Blotting-paper Style," *Times Literary Supplement*, 20 November 1970, p. 1346.
9. Quoted in J. B. Pick, "The Work of David Lindsay," *Studies in Scottish Literature*, 1 (1964), p. 172.
10. Arthur Schopenhauer, *The World as Will and Idea*, translated by R. B. Haldane and J. Kemp (London: Trench, 1909), III, p. 26.
11. Ibid., I, p. 410.
12. *A Voyage to Arcturus* (New York: Ballantine, 1968), p. 287. All future page references to *A Voyage to Arcturus* will be given in the text and will refer to this most recent and widely available paperback edition.
13. Gerard Sitwell, *"The Cloud of Unknowing,"* in *English Spiritual Writers*, ed. Charles Davis (New York: Sheed and Ward, 1961), pp. 41–50.
14. Erich Neumann, *The Origins and History of Consciousness*, trans. R. F. C. Hull (New York: Harper Torchbooks, 1962), p. 297.
15. C. S. Lewis, "On Stories," in *Of Other Worlds*, ed. Walter Hooper (New York: Harcourt, Brace, and World, 1966), p. 12.
16. Quoted in Pick, "Work of David Lindsay," p. 179.
17. George MacDonald, *Phantastes and Lilith*, p. 13.
18. Quoted in Pick, "Sketch," in *Strange Genius of David Lindsay*, p. 26.
19. Lewis, p. 12.
20. Quoted in Pick, "Sketch," in *Strange Genius of David Lindsay*, p. 13.
21. Schopenhauer, I, p. 202.

22. Ibid., III, p. 37.
23. *Beyond Good and Evil*, trans. Walter Kaufmann (New York: Vintage, 1966), pp. 145–146. Quoted in Mensing's "Introduction," *A Voyage to Arcturus* (Boston: Gregg Press, 1977), p. viii.
24. *Beyond Good and Evil*, quoted in Mensing, p. x.
25. Mensing, p. xi.
26. Neumann, p. 156.
27. Nietzche, *The Gay Science*, quoted by Mensing, p. xii.
28. *The Birth of Tragedy*, quoted in Mensing, p. xi.
29. Mensing, p. xiii.
30. Schopenhauer, III, p. 313.
31. *The Younger Edda of Snorre Sturleson*, translated by I. A. Blackwell (London: Norroena Society, 1907), p. 335.
32. Quoted in Pick, "Sketch," in *Strange Genius of David Lindsay*.
33. Quoted in Pick, "Work of David Lindsay," p. 175.
34. *The Younger Edda . . .*, p. 260.
35. Ibid., p. 343.

IV

THE HAUNTED WOMAN

Like George MacDonald before him, Lindsay was disappointed in the reception of his first major work of fantasy and feared that the few who had read it misunderstood it. MacDonald waited nearly forty years before returning to the genre he had pioneered with *Phantastes* in 1858 (*Lilith* appeared in 1895), building a successful career in the meantime as a writer of more realistic romances and novels, as well as several children's stories and fairy tales. But Lindsay seemed to feel that he must get his vision before the public again, and he lacked both the temperament and the novelistic skill to turn from it in favor of more ordinary kinds of fiction. After *Arcturus,* however, he never again returned to the wildly inventive epic landscapes and adventures that had made that work so striking. There are indeed passages in later works—particularly *Devil's Tor* and *The Witch* —that echo the imaginative power of *Arcturus,* but for the most part Lindsay sought means to present his ideas in forms more closely approaching what he believed his readers' expectations to be—and that meant writing novels that were by and large confined to reasonably familiar earthly settings, that developed characters more fully, and that dealt in some detail with the surface social relationships among these characters. None of these areas, unfortunately, quite coincided with Lindsay's strengths as a writer. His fictional conversations are stilted and full of philosophical exposition unrelated to the nominal narrative action, his descriptions of characters crude and tactless, his narratives overly detailed and slow-moving. Yet these later works remain strange and fascinating fictions—in some ways more fascinating than *Arcturus* itself, for they offer many of the same philosophical challenges as that masterpiece without providing us with the diversion of such rich fantastic invention. These later novels not only illuminate *Arcturus,* they bring us more closely in contact with the philosophical notions that are at the center of Lindsay's thought, and, for the student of fantasy, they offer interesting studies in the problems of constructing plausible philosophical fictions, fictions in which the fantastic elements grow naturally out of the ideational structures and in which the ideas seem to demand fantasy images.

Lindsay's second published work was *The Haunted Woman* (1922), a slight and delicate love story which details the three-week relationship between a young lady named Isbel Loment and an embittered older man named Henry Judge, whose house she is considering buying. Though Isbel is engaged to an underwriter, Marshall Stokes, she and Judge are attracted to one another at some elemental level, but social convention and their own inhibitions prevent each of them from acknowledging the attraction. But in Runhill, Judge's ancestral home, is an ancient secret room known as "Ulf's Tower," named, according to legend, after a sixth-century Saxon named Ulf who built the original house on the site or Runhill. The area was reputedly haunted by trolls, and Ulf himself—along with the tower portion of his house—mysteriously disappeared one morning, supposedly carted off by the trolls. For a sensitive few, however, the tower reappears occasionally and may be entered by means of a phantom staircase that also appears at these intervals. Both Isbel and Henry are among the few capable of entering the tower, and when they meet there, the inhibitions of the outer world are stripped away, and they become capable of expressing their true love for one another.

But the room has another magical quality: those who do enter it later have no memory of having been there or of anything that happened there. Thus, while Isbel and Henry are capable of declaring their love in the phantom room, when they return to the outside world they remain only vaguely aware of some special relationship they seem to enjoy; and when Isbel gives Henry her scarf during their first encounter in the room, neither of them are later able to explain the circumstances under which he came into its possession.

It would be easy at this point to assume that the room is a purely psychological symbol, that it is an abode of the subconscious just as the outer world of social graces is the abode of the conscious. But there is more to the room than the stripping away of social facades. The room is also the gateway to a different world, a youthful world of apparently eternal spring, of natural landscapes uncluttered by the intrusions of man. (As we shall see in *Devil's Tor*, Lindsay apparently regarded the artificial structures of man as an excrescence on the true world of nature.) This world appears to be governed by a mysterious musician whose face is never seen, but whose powerful lute melodies recall the emotionally devastating music of Earthrid in *A Voyage to Arcturus*. Not everyone can survive the elemental emotions of this world, pleasant though they seem to Henry and Isbel. When a medium named Mrs. Richborough stumbles into the room, the experience virtually destroys all the values of gossip and meddlesomeness that she has lived by. " 'All that state of mind seems suddenly so trivial and unimportant,' " she comments.[1] Not long after her experience in the room, the terrified and distraught Mrs. Richborough dies.

Concerned by the death of Mrs. Richborough and what he suspects is a connection between her death and her experience in the phantom room, Henry suggests that he and Isbel end their relationship, at least for the time being, and leaves a letter for her at the hotel where he has been staying, giving no forwarding address. As Isbel leaves the hotel, however, she catches sight of an apparition: Mrs. Richborough, seated in a car, ordering the driver to Runhill Court. Puzzled and not a little suspicious, Isbel follows the car to Runhill, and there meets Henry for the last time, on the pathway leading to the house. It is a grey, misty day, but for Henry it is the landscape of spring in Ulf's world—for he has gone up the phantom staircase and not come back. Henry tries to bring Isbel into this world— he plays music for her, he exhorts her to exert her will to deny the drab reality that surrounds her—and for a few moments she is able to glimpse the springtime landscape that he inhabits. A kind of battle for her consciousness ensues between the two worlds: the one a world of drab mists, hypocrisies, and social conventions; the other a world of intense passion and pain and stark clarity. Perhaps because she is unaided by the special magic of Ulf's tower or perhaps because her will is not sufficiently strong to overcome the reality that surrounds her, Isbel cannot sustain her vision of the other world, and in a final flash of clarity she sees the figure of Henry standing on a hillside, looking into the face of the mysterious musician whose back remains to her:

> His back was turned towards her, so that she could not see his face, but Henry, who was standing erect and motionless beyond, was looking right into it, and, from his expression, it was as though he were beholding some appalling vision! . . . She screamed and ran towards him, calling him by name. Before she had taken three steps, however, the musician jerked his whole force savagely into his bow-arm, and she was brought up with a violent shock. Such sharp brutality of passion she had never heard expressed by any sound. . . . The sunlight grew suddenly hotter and darker, the landscape appeared to close rapidly in upon her, some catastrophe was impending; her blood was boiling and freezing. . . .
>
> At that moment it seemed to her that yonder strange man was the centre around which everything in the landscape was moving, and that she herself was no more than his *dream*! . . .
>
> And then Henry's face was crossed by an expression of sickness; he changed colour; she caught a faint groan, and directly afterwards he sank helplessly to the ground, where he continued lying quite still. . . . She stood paralyzed, staring in horror . . . (pp. 167–168).

Isbel's vision disappears, the mists close in on her again, and she faints. The next day, Marshall Stokes, who has grown suspicious of Isbel's relationship with Henry, visits Runhill and finds Henry dead in the East Room—the room in which the magical staircase had materialized for Henry and Isbel. Isbel and Marshall end their engagement, and some time later Isbel finds that Marshall is beginning to fall in love with her close friend, Blanche.

Certain stylistic problems plague Lindsay from the outset of this novel. For the character relationships he sets up to be believable, he needs to gear his style more effectively to the emotional tone of each scene. But Lindsay's style moves with almost the same harsh precision, only slightly tempered, that characterizes *A Voyage to Arcturus* and that gives even that work the superficial appearance of mechanical allegory. Lindsay seems to lack the essential sympathy for his characters that would seem to be a prerequisite for writing a love story. Witness the initial description of Isbel, for example:

> Her face was rather short and broad, with thick but sensitive features, a lowish forehead, and a dull, heavy skin, rendered almost unnaturally pale by the excessive quantity of powder she employed. . . . The full, grey-black eyes, as a rule, appeared a trifle bored and absent, but occasionally they narrowed into a subtle and penetrating glance which

nearly resembled a stab. Her hair was long and fine, but mouse-colored. She was short, rather than tall, and somewhat too broad-hipped for modern ideas of beauty; nevertheless her person was graceful and well-covered . . . (p. 8).

Certain of these characteristics, such as the "excessive quantity of powder," help us to understand Isbel's character and the extent of her immersion in a world of illusion and false faces; but the overall carryover from *A Voyage to Arcturus* of the vocabulary of ugliness—"thick," "lowish," "dull, heavy," "stab," "mouse-colored," etc.—does little service to the woman who is to be the protagonist and love-object of the story (although it must be admitted that Lindsay's entire view of the phenomenal world seems bathed in such images). Other aspects of the description seem merely poor writing: "She was short, rather than tall" is tautological, while her "penetrating glance" appears "occasionally" for no discernible reason that relates either to her character or to events at hand. Lindsay's "realistic" characterizations often give this impression of being assorted queer characteristics arbitrarily bundled together and given suggestive names. Though the names are in no way as provocative as the names in *A Voyage to Arcturus*, they are still intriguing: "Loment," for example, suggests both "lament" and the Latin word for face cream, *lomentum,* either of which would be appropriate for Isbel's character.

But beyond considerations of style and character, Lindsay's central problems seem to arise from attempting to cast his novel in a realistic mode at all. The reader is drawn to Ulf's world and wants to learn more about it—and Lindsay himself seems far more fascinated by this world than by the "real" one, but he deliberately confines our views of it to a few quick glances and explains nothing. Thus, we are left to make what we can of the more detailed picture of Edwardian country life that he gives us and to wonder how this world relates to the far more powerful and interesting vision that is largely withheld from us. It appears likely that Lindsay, in *The Haunted Woman*, is attempting to illustrate by specific example the dangers that this web of illusion we live in can pose to individual human relationships and the tragedy that can result. Instead of Crystalman's world, we have the world of social convention and propriety, represented by Isbel's engagement to Stokes, her wardship under Mrs. Moor, and her "old school tie" with her friend Blanche. All these relationships are artificial and restrictive, and each involve people willfully manipulating others. But such relationships are necessary for the social structure to survive, if only because, as Judge says, men and women are " 'so anxious to be deceived' " (p. 62). In Ulf's world, the deceptions are lifted, and individuals are forced to confront the reality of themselves. It is possible, as E. H. Visiak suggests, that Ulf is the Crystalman of this world,[2] but Lindsay clearly suggests that even if Ulf's world is illusory, it is closer to reality than the world of acceptable social behavior.

As in *A Voyage to Arcturus*, the reality principle of the other world is signalized by music. The image of the disappearing staircase is first suggested to Isbel by the introduction to Beethoven's Seventh Symphony, which she hears played on the piano by a visiting American when she first visits Runhill:

> She knew the composition well, but had never heard it played like that before. The disturbing excitement of its preparations, as if a curtain were about to be drawn up, revealing a new and marvelous world. . . . It was wonderful . . . most beautiful, really. . . . Then, after a few minutes came the famous passage of the gigantic ascending scales, and she immediately had a vision of huge stairs going up . . . (p. 27).

Later Sherrup, the American, explains that " 'Some ideas came to me in this house which seemed to require music to illustrate them—that particular music, I mean' " (p. 29). Shortly afterward, in the upstairs corridor of the house, Isbel experiences her first direct sensations of the other world: she hears a sound described variously as " 'a kind of low, vibrating hum' " (p. 33), " 'like an orchestra heard through a thick wall' " (p. 34), or " 'like the far-away scrape of a double-bass' " (p. 40). None of Isbel's companions can hear this sound, but Sherrup has heard it and experienced a strange springtime odor as well. Both he and Isbel agree that the sound seems to come from another world and that it suggests some impending event of great magnitude. But Sherrup failed to get the image of a staircase from the music, perhaps indicating that, though sensitive, he is not as attuned to the music of Ulf's world as Isbel is.

Later, music plays an increasingly important role in the narrative. When Isbel first meets Judge in the phantom room, she comments that " 'The air here seems different. It's nobler, and there's sort of music in it' " (p. 85). When, on a later visit to the room, the two of them hear Ulf's music directly, the melody appears to be an early-English air "which was altogether beyond the range of the understanding and seemed to belong to other days, when feelings were more poignant and delicate, less showy, splendid, and odourless" (p. 127). The pure passion of this music impressed them both, and Henry comments, " 'Music must have been like that at one time' " (p. 133). A still later occurrence of the music has an even more dramatic effect on Isbel:

> She felt suddenly that she had up to now been playing with life, but that reality had at length clutched her in its grim grasp, and now she must show what stuff she was made of. She was like a bather for whom a river proves too strong, and who is being walked downstream step by step, struggling in vain for footholds, until her waist is covered, and she must either swim or resign herself to be carried away to death. . . . Her old happiness was past recovery. It rested with herself whether she were to be borne along backwards, looking after it despairingly, or whether she should throw herself audaciously into this new element, confiding in her strength and courage to bring her to safety. . . . She realized that this was the moment she had been waiting for all her life . . . (p. 137).

Lest we feel that this music is all life and romance, however, we must remember that it is also the musician who seems responsible for Henry's death, which occurs at the moment of a particular violent passage played by the mysterious figure. Music, which expresses no meaning other than itself, becomes for Lindsay the only truly appropriate image from the phenomenal world for the absolute reality of passion and will that he seeks to express.

If the themes of passion, will, and reality in *The Haunted Woman* seem in large measure to be restatements of the same themes in *A Voyage to Arcturus*, there are also themes in this second novel that were not as deeply explored in the first and that look forward instead to Lindsay's later works. Foremost among these is the theme of men-women relationships. *A Voyage to Arcturus* had hinted at the powerful role of sexuality in human behavior with the character of Sullenbode and of the different reality perceived by women and men in the character of Gleameil, but the novel did not directly address the problem of romance, and in many ways this is the central issue that Isbel faces in *The Haunted Woman*. The title of the novel is interesting in this respect, since to all outward appearances it is the estate of Runhill that is haunted or perhaps the hill on which Runhill was built (we are even told this directly, in the legend of Ulf). But Lindsay did not call his novel *The Haunted Manor* or *The Haunted Hillside*, suggesting that the word "woman" is a key term in the title. Precisely *why* is Isbel haunted, and what is it that haunts her?

The key to much of this comes in a dinner-party scene early in the novel, where Isbel emerges as a woman struggling with the conflicts that arise from her assigned role in society, her conditioned ideas of romance, and her growing sense of a deeper reality that makes the other conditions increasingly unsatisfying. Isbel also emerges as a rather prescient advocate of feminism—prescient at least for a character in a novel written by an Englishman in 1922. When Henry comments that " 'many of the cleverest women in history have been the most fascinating,' " Isbel retorts with the comment, " 'But history has been written by men, and men aren't the most enlightened critics where women are concerned. All that will have to be re-written by qualified feminine experts some day' " (p. 62). Judge goes on to argue that men actually make better critics of women than other women, for men tend to look for noble qualities where other women seek to find faults. Again Isbel retorts: " 'It may be very chivalrous, but I don't call it criticism. . . . You're not in the least likely ever to understand a woman's character that way' " (p. 62).

As the discussion progresses, it becomes apparent that Isbel and Henry, for all their differences, are each looking for something deeper in their relationships than proper society has to offer. Real love, argues Judge, " 'would be the most difficult thing in the world to simulate. . . if only men and women were not so anxious to be deceived' " (p. 62). The deception, of course, is that the relatively shallow emotions that pass for love in the world are the real thing. Henry goes on to explain that this feeling he describes is not what is commonly thought of as "romance": " 'There are deep, and possibly painful, transactions of the heart to which the term "romance" would be quite inadequate.' " Isbel quickly recognizes that " 'it can't be a happy condition—this deep passion you have just described' " (p. 63). Henry agrees, but adds that few by nature ever experience such passion, " 'and there's no reason for anyone to suppose that he or she is one of the tragic band. The chances are infinitely against it' " (p. 64).

Isbel, of course, is one of the "tragic band," as is Judge, and her strength of character is an early indication of this. She demands to be treated as an individual, not, as the current phrase has it, a "sex-object." When one of the dinner guests proposes a verse for the occasion based on Omar Khayyam's "a jug of wine, a loaf of bread, and thou," Isbel quickly responds, " 'I strongly protest against figuring in it as a 'thou'. . . . Those times are past for ever. Henceforward men are going to exist for us, not we for them' " (p. 73). Isbel is seeking a deeper reality than society will allow her, and it is ironic that when she expresses a desire for friends at this deeper level, " 'friends who aren't afraid of giving,' " one of the other dinner guests accuses her of suffering from " 'acute *romance*. Such interesting persons no longer walk this hard, cold world of ours, if they have ever done so. A man's best friend is his bank-balance. You may take that as an axiom' " (p. 74). Isbel, aware of the irony in this remark, agrees wholeheartedly. Lindsay makes a key point in this passage about his own work and ideas, as well: those who seek a reality deeper than that acknowledged by social conventions are apt to be regarded as romantics by those who can see no such deeper reality.

It would thus be a mistake to regard *The Haunted Woman* as merely a pale reflection of the vision of *A Voyage to Arcturus*. Certainly the novel is tame by comparison to that earlier work, but it also introduces new themes and ideas that Lindsay will develop in later novels, such as *Devil's Tor* and *The Witch*. Furthermore, it provides us with a clearer view of how Lindsay's philosophical ideas impact on our social behavior and adds a depth of psychological insight to the relatively abstract philosophical propositions that governed *A Voyage to Arcturus*. It also, not incidentally, establishes Lindsay as a precursor of writers who would later deal with feminist ideas and values; Isbel is probably the strongest independent female character, who is neither a great mother nor a romantic ideal, to appear in English fantasy writing up to this time. As a human character, she is one of Lindsay's most complex and fully realized creations, haunted by a vision of something deeper than that which life offers her and in the end, after Henry's death, punished for this vision by being left alone by those who are more easily satisfied. Like Maskull in *A Voyage to Arcturus*, she has seen a deeper reality than most of us experience, and she has returned changed. A comment early in the novel by Priday, the caretaker of Runhill, foreshadows Isbel's fate and provides an appropriate epigraph for her, for Maskull, and possibly for Lindsay himself: " 'P'raps those who start a funny journey can't always come back when they like' " (p. 47).

Notes

1. *The Haunted Woman* (London: Gollancz, 1964), p. 125. Future references will be to this edition.
2. E. H. Visiak, "The Haunted Woman," in *The Strange Genius of David Lindsay* (London: John Baker, 1970), p. 108.

V

DEVIL'S TOR

Lindsay began work on what would eventually become the last novel he was to publish during his lifetime as early as 1922. Originally titled "The Ancient Tragedy" (a title whose meaning remains evident in the published version), the novel was rejected by a series of publishers in the early twenties. In 1928, Lindsay began an extensive revision and rewriting, changing the title to *Devil's Tor*, and, with the aid of influential friends, finally placing the novel with Putnam's in 1932. By the time *Devil's Tor* was published, Lindsay had not published a novel in more than five years and was becoming increasingly embittered about his failure to find an audience. This sense of failure is apparent in the novel: it is certainly the most uncompromising and difficult of all the works published during his lifetime, and much of this difficulty seems to arise from his lack of concessions to the reader. The pacing of the novel is excruciatingly slow, the style often completely out of control, the characterizations harsh and unengaging, and the ideas obtuse and relentlessly detailed. But the work is as rich in ideas as *A Voyage to Arcturus,* and if the reader approaches it as a philosophical disquisition rather than as a series of actions, it can be among the most rewarding and fascinating of Lindsay's books.

Lindsay's own account of the novel, written in a letter to his publisher, provides a concise summary of what he was attempting:

> *Devil's Tor* was conceived in a spirit of music . . . To the curious in such matters I should have to refer *Devil's Tor*, as to its primary origins, not to any master of prose, living or dead, but to the tremendous creator of the Ninth Symphony. The first movement of that work has generally been more or less in my head during the book's writing.
>
> But the story's actual themes—Fate made visible, the Great Mother, the mystic stones belonging to a world of other dimensions, the part of the Northern races in history, the supernatural bringing-together of a chosen pair for the uplifting of humanity, the purpose of the creation of the universes—these belong not to one time or one mental birth, but have been built up of infinite darkness and confusion. The eye caring to discern will see in them the evident traces of an astronomical parallax: by which I mean a progress of the story, not only from the first chapter to the last, but across the sky-space of thought itself.[1]

It is apparent that Lindsay has chosen vast themes for his novel, and indeed he does treat of the purpose of the world, the nature of fate, the evolution of the human races, the origin of religions, and the function of art! He has attempted to encompass all these themes and more in a story as simple on the surface as that of *The Haunted Woman:* the story of the discovery and eventual bringing together of two halves of a mystical stone which had been broken in distant antiquity (the "ancient tragedy," presumably, of the novel's original title).

To focus these various ideas and themes, Lindsay offers one concession that he did not offer in his earlier books: he casts his myth in the framework of a great public myth that, in part at least, is familiar to most readers. This is the myth of the Great Mother, Goethe's "eternal feminine," though Lindsay's use of this myth does not draw only from Goethe and Schopenhauer, but also from a formidable body of learning and speculation in anthropology, history, and religion. Many of Lindsay's notions even anticipate the role of the Great Mother in later Jungian psychology; in any event, *Devil's Tor* almost certainly represents the most detailed working out of this myth in all of literary fantasy.

Lindsay finds manifestations of the Great Mother in all aspects of life and history. First, and most evidently, she is in nature—but only dimly realized in a nature that man has systematically demythified through his science and degraded through his art and industry. Early in the novel, the character Hugh Drapier comes to realize this:

> First, Nature lived with and dimly apprehended through a veil of glory; the gods and goddesses, witches, elves and fairies. Then the transition; the Almighty and His saints, speaking the language of the Cross. And lastly the fully-emancipated intellect, finding itself amazed in a fearful life without personal future, for which it had never asked.
>
> Arsinal's "Great Mother"—she was Nature, when men had been children. She was dead. Men themselves had killed her. Or could she conceivably rise again in the fashion of a dead god?[2]

(Arsinal is a scholar who has traced the myth of the Great Mother through many cultures.) Drapier feels that man, with his "houses, pavements, factories, mines, quarries, cuttings, bridges, railways, cars, engines and machinery, slag-heaps, gas-works, roads, stagnant canals" and so on, has undertaken a systematic "assassination of Nature" by reducing it to his own base terms and that the most powerful force in this direction has been the rise of democracy. "The infinitely greater weight of the mass nowadays was an irresistible force pulling men towards each other and away from the lonely Austere and Sublime. The other name of this gravitation was democracy; so that democracy was the grand evil" (pp. 68-69; Chapter VI). Later, Arsinal explains that such a tendency in man may be the result of his primitive fear of nature during an earlier stage of civilization (Chapter XXVII, p. 402).

If nature is a manifestation of the Great Mother, it follows that art, which is a reflection of nature, should be another manifestation. Magnus Colborne, an aging writer and uncle of the novel's heroine, explains:

> Whatever on earth is of softness, sweetness, fineness, fairness, delicacy, aerial lightness, has derived from a feminine, not a masculine, source. The pleasing forms and colours of the painting art, the thrilling sensuous progression of musical tones, the haunting chains of poetry—they too are feminine. The very spirit that incites to the arts is feminine. . . . Subtract women, babes, beauty, love, Nature, civilisation, the arts, from life; what is there left? A workshop and a battlefield. . . .
> . . . —it has never ceased to be understood by the senses of man,

following upon his partial emancipation from the naked passions of sex, that this *Ewigweibliche* is immediately responsible for the construction of this the physical, mental, moral and spiritual universe through which we painfully wander, as in a dream (Chapter XII, pp. 158–159).

In art as in nature, then, we catch a glimpse of the eternal feminine, the *Ewigweibliche,* as a unity—as, in fact, *the* unity from which all diversity has sprung. Another possible meaning of "the ancient tragedy" is the dissolution of this primal unity through its "fall" into sex. Femaleness, Lindsay argues, transcends what we know as sexuality and existed before sexual differentiation came into the world. This is the insight by an artist named Peter Copping near the end of the book:

> So he too came to conceive how femaleness could be before sex. Existing alone, needing no completing half, marvellously wise, solitary, ancient, awful, the *female* had in some unthinkable hour of cosmic tragedy fallen into sex, thereafter to become the slave and sport of its derivative. Thus the unnatural effeminacies of women, their animal voluptuousness and cowardly sheltering from the knocks of the world, their infantine love of dress, their intense interest in the interrelations of men and women, their passion to outvie other women in wealth, rank, influence, society, and beauty: all came from that fall to sex. But the heights of woman were original. In nobler purity she was once a whole nature (Chapter XXXI, pp. 452–453).

Though the unity of the eternal feminine may have been lost in the fall to sex, there have remained throughout history individual women, both real and mythical, who have been associated with this unity. " 'A line of phenomenal women has always existed in the world,' " Copping says (Chapter X, p. 136). (And Lindsay was to devote his last unfinished novel, *The Witch*, to further exploring the nature of such women.) In Christian mythology, the earliest such avatar of the feminine was of course Eve. Saltfleet, who more or less emerges as the novel's hero, at one point arrives at an unusual interpretation of Genesis in light of this feminine principle:

> Eve, not eating of the fruit, must have remained the simple insipid female of her species; but the serpent, who surely was God disguised, persuaded her to her fiercer, higher heart, when instantly her immortal soul could know both itself and the horror of her unreal body (Chapter XXVIII, p. 410).

This passage should provide a cautionary note to any reading tempted to equate Lindsay's "fall into sex" with the Christian fall from grace. The fall into sex, he clearly implies here and elsewhere in the novel, must have taken place at a far earlier stage of evolution than even the Genesis myth.

But by far the most widely evident avatar of the Great Mother in Christian culture is the figure of Mary, and Mary is the most widely discussed such figure in the novel. Early on, Magnus Colborne speculates on why the figure of Mary, " 'almost the most inconspicuous leading figure in the Gospel " (Chapter XI, p. 154), should be the most widely represented figure in Christian art and carry more emotional "force" in her representations than all the angels, saints, martyrs, or Christ himself. The reason, he suggests, is that " 'the human instinct is more powerful far than the human reason' " (Chapter XI, p. 154) and that man instinctively moves toward the feminine and not toward such later intellectual constructions as are represented by other Christian icons. Mary " 'joins the infinite and the finite,' " says Colborne, " 'she is at once a person and a principle.' "

> We are in a world, the whole significance of which is womanly. We are born of a woman, woman's blood is in us, we sever ourselves from the womanly at the high cost of becoming brutal, or denatured, or grey, dry and old before our time—our moments of greatest rapture, as well, are on account of a woman, and when we die, it is not bearded faces that we desire to see around our bed. The world belongs to women; not to us (Chapter XII, p. 159).

Arsinal, the scholar, has traced the myth of the Virgin through many cultures and finds that it often antedates the story of Christ (Chapter XX). Christ, he suspects (as Colborne had suspected earlier in the novel), represents an attempt fairly late in the history of the myth to graft onto it principles associated with male dominance. The result, Arsinal feels, is doomed to failure, and he sees the worship of Christ steadily in decline.

> The attempted paintings of the adult Christ—they have not contented anyone: lachrymose, cadaverous, *undivine*, they have been on a parity with His whole impossibility. For two genders have had to be reconciled within His person; and each has had to be absolute: the man and male god, the law-dispenser, stern, rigid, awful; but also the womanly spring of that love, compassion, and purity, that only in the female nature seem to be original; in males, derived—an act of will, an effort (Chapter XXVII, p. 403).

The androgynous Christ, then, represents an attempt to reconcile man's will to power with the more humane qualities traditionally associated with the eternal feminine; but Lindsay, apparently, does not allow for such a synthesis—not in this world, at least.

Lindsay's treatment of the Great Mother myth is so thorough that he even offers a plausible, non-mystical hypothesis for the origins of the myth. Arsinal surmises that the worship of womanhood dates from a period before the earliest communities, when isolated tribes and families, " 'constantly threatened by the overwhelming perils of a terrible natural world,' " were not large enough for the men to trust the protection of women even in part to the community. As a result, " 'each man must defend his own, and such defense, from love, becomes reverence' " (Chapter XXIII, p. 334).

As though the Great Mother myth by itself were not sufficient to support all of Lindsay's ideas in this novel, he combines it with an odd mystique of race that was almost certainly influenced by Nietzsche but that seems curiously at odds with Lindsay's other statements on the subject. According to Arsinal, the blue-eyed Nordic races are somehow associated in its origins with an ancient meteorite, and that extraterrestrial powers associated with this meteorite gave unusual creative powers to these peoples. The "blue-eyed" peoples began in Northwest Europe (possibly on Devil's Tor itself), but they branched out and influenced culture throughout the world. Later blue-eyed peoples descended from this common stock included the Norse, the early Romans, the Achaeans, and the Celts, according to Arsinal. " 'It is no conjecture, but necessity, that these blue-eyed peoples, appearing suddenly as strangers in a world of brown humanity, should be derived from one stock' " (Chapter XXIII, p. 329). Much of the art and culture in the world derives from these northern races: " 'but for those successive bands of furious blue-eyed potential lords, and kings, and feudal landowners, the temples of Greece and the Gothic cathedrals could never have arisen' " (Chapter XVI, p. 227), argues Arsinal, and he goes on to credit these races with the temples of Karnak, the pyramids, and even Hindu philosophy! " 'The sublime philosophies of India represent the turned ebb of such a tide of blue-eyed warriors sweeping in from the west' " (Chapter XX, p. 273). Other races, says Arsinal, have achieved nothing of significance:

> The Chinese and Japanese have given us decorative forms of art that could not rise to sublimity. . . . No dark-skinned race has yet achieved a philosophy; for the Upanishads of India are from the Aryans. The Jews and Arabs have willed, rather than meditated, their sullen monotheistic systems, and these systems have remained barbaric, of blood and towards blood (Chapter XXIII, p. 333).

Why Lindsay felt such racist attitudes necessary for his narrative is puzzling, but before we leap to the conclusion that such attitudes are Lindsay's own, we should keep in mind that the character Arsinal is the exclusive spokesman for these attitudes. At one point he is even undercut in his theorizing by the skeptical Saltfleet, who interrupts Arsinal's rambling about " 'blue-eyed, deep-thoughted, metaphysical giants' " to observe that " 'pure blonds are still frequent enough; whereas my experience is that they are usually of the sportsman type, and spiritually rather peculiarly phlegmatic' " (Chapter XX, p. 273). Arsinal can only counter with a lame observation that the truth of science is rarely to be found on the surface. Furthermore, in Lindsay's own early notes for the novel, he had expressed a quite different attitude toward racial purity:

> Pure breeds and races of mankind stand to cross-breeds in the same relation as the animal species stand to man in general. They are stationary and crystallised; no longer in the main trend of progress. The cross-breed is the free and fluid creature, from whom all is to be hoped. It follows that the nationalities and the patriotism that attends nationalities, are inconsistent with fundamental freedom and progress.[3]

This suggests that we should be cautious in attributing Arsinal's beliefs, extensively expounded as they are in the novel, with Lindsay's own.

When the "new race" is to be created after the joining of the mystical stones at the end of the novel, the parents are Ingrid Fleming, who is a "pure Nordic type," and Henry Saltfleet, who is described as florid, grey-eyed, and resembling the Roman dictator Sulla.

Given this vast metaphysical backdrop, Lindsay's plot seems slight indeed, especially for a novel that approaches five hundred pages in length. The story opens with an adventurer named Hugh Drapier arriving to visit his cousin Ingrid Fleming, her mother Helga, and her uncle Magnus Colborne, at their isolated home on the Dartmoor moors. Drapier has been drawn to Dartmoor following an adventure in Tibet in which two other explorers, fleeing the natives, entrusted to him a curious flint that they had stolen from a sacred shrine. The flint, which somehow seems to reflect the skies of another world, begins to exercise strange powers over Drapier: he has premonitions of his own death, he is powerfully attracted to a nearby outcropping of stone called Devil's Tor, and he increasingly finds the prospect of returning the stone to those who had entrusted it to him distasteful.

Drapier visits Devil's Tor with Ingrid, and during a fierce thunderstorm, a bolt of lightning dislodges the devil's head stone that gives the tor its name, exposing a vast underground tomb. Ingrid has a momentary vision of an enormous woman (sooner or later, just about everybody who visits the Tor has such a vision; there are more than fifteen such visions described in the book, and Ingrid herself has about four of them). The next day, Drapier returns to explore the tomb, but breaks his flashlight and stumbles in the darkness. His hand closes on a small stone, which he later assumes to be the flint from Tibet, fallen from his pocket. It is not, of course; it is instead the matching other half of the stone, separated from its mate eons earlier.

Most of the next four hundred pages or so are spent trying to get the two halves of the mystical stone back together, and Lindsay goes to lengths worthy of a Restoration dramatist to keep them apart for this length of time. When Hugh returns to the house and finds the stone missing from the box in which he had placed it, he takes this as evidence that he had inadvertently carried it with him into the tomb, dropped it, and picked it up again. Actually Helga, Ingrid's mother, had become fascinated with his original stone and temporarily purloined it.

When Hugh leaves the tomb the second time, an earth tremor collapses it for good, the suggestion being that such a coincidence of natural disasters could only be the result of the same supernatural forces that drew Hugh to Dartmoor in the first place and that are associated with the mysterious stones. Meanwhile, the two explorers from Tibet, Henry Saltfleet and Stephen Arsinal, arrive in the neighborhood, prepared at all costs to retrieve the flint they believe is rightfully theirs. Saltfleet, an experienced Tibetan climber and explorer retained by Arsinal in his quest for a mysterious stone said to be associated with the Great Mother myth, arrives first. In two chapters of digressive flashback (Chapters 15 and 16), we learn of Arsinal's extensive researches and his quest for the mother-stone. Lindsay is not inaccurate in associating the myth of the Great

Mother with flint stones; Erich Neumann observed that "it is no accident that 'stones' are among the oldest symbols of the Great Mother Goddess. . . . The Great Earth Mother is the mother of stones, of stone implements, and of fire."[4] Much of the fictional scholarship of Arsinal, in fact, seems to remarkably anticipate the later researches of Neumann and others.

Arsinal has discovered two ancient inscriptions which seem to attest to the existence of the stones and their power. The first, a Minoan tablet found at Knossos, reads in part:

> "That which came from the stars, and is full of words of its home. That which unwillingly flees from its bride in the west. That which has ever brought fulfillment and ill-hap to him who has borne it. That which the seer has said shall know no change until that it has united another man and another woman, of whom shall be born a son greater than they, greater than all mankind, who shall be the saviour" (Chapter XVI, p. 224).

The second inscription, from a silver figurine of the mother goddess found in Aphrodisias in Caria, reads " ' "To one bed shall I bring another man and another woman, of whom shall be born a greater than they, greater than all mankind, who shall put wickedness underfoot, and found my people" ' " (Chapter XX, p. 269).

Clearly, the bringing of the two stones together is to result in the founding of a new race on earth. The only question remaining is, who shall be the chosen couple? Saltfleet begins negotiating for the return of the stone first with Helga and later with Peter Copping, an artist who is Ingrid's fiancee. But when he visits the Tor to find Drapier, who has returned there for a third time, he finds him dead, the stone clutched in his hand. He takes the stone and returns to show it to Arsinal, who proclaims it is not his stone at all, but rather its mate. The original is still in Ingrid's house. After some absurdly detailed legalistic quibbling as to which stone belongs properly to whom, Saltfleet and Arsinal set up a meeting with Copping and Ingrid on Devil's Tor, for the purpose of joining the two stones. By this time it is apparent that Ingrid, the "pure Nordic type," is to be the chosen mother of the new race, but which of the three men on the Tor will be its father? The answer may reveal something further of Lindsay's philosophy, especially in regard to intellect, art, and action.

Arsinal does not seem a likely candidate, for his role in the novel seems clearly defined as the theorist who discovers the importance of the stones and initiates the quest for them. Just as Drapier functions primarily as the agent for uncovering the second stone, so Arsinal functions as the agent for finding the first. " 'For a man who is neither prophet, nor reformer, nor deliverer,' " he says of himself, " 'it may be a sufficiently worthy labour to rescue from the defiling dust a divine shape of antiquity, though it be not of marble or bronze' " (Chapter XV, p. 218). Though he too experiences visions, he does not fully understand them (his principal vision on the Tor is of a prehistoric worship service of the Great Mother among a tribe of pre-humans). He is the man of intellect, and the intellect alone is insufficient for the creation of a new world.

Peter Copping, the artist, in this final meeting on the Tor perceives a strange gleaming in Ingrid and Saltfleet that Arsinal does not see, "because it was a spiritual light, not for the conceited simplicity of the eye of the brain thinking to construct everything from surfaces" (Chapter XXXII, p. 462). Copping, the intuitive artist, comes much closer to being able to understand the visions he receives and often seems to speak for Lindsay himself—at least as far as Lindsay's views of art are concerned. Earlier in the novel, for example, Copping had spoken of symbols and allegories in a manner that seems a direct response of Lindsay to those who persist in reading his books as allegories. " 'Allegories!' " he says. " 'The symbol and the allegory. Yet there remain quite well-educated persons who definitely don't know one from the other. A symbol is a mystic sign of the Creator. An allegory is a wall decoration with a label attached' " (Chapter XI, p. 145). But as Peter understands art, he also understands its limitations, and early on he senses that Ingrid may be drawn to something higher than he can offer and suggests that their engagement be made conditional on nothing unusual happening for a year. Peter recognizes, but does not fully understand, what is happening between Ingrid and Saltfleet on the Tor. He says to Ingrid, " 'You are Hers—not mine' " (Chapter XXXI, p. 459), and departs the hill.

This leaves Saltfleet, the man of action, the synthesis of the intellect and the feeling, to be Ingrid's chosen husband—though neither he nor Ingrid do the choosing. Saltfleet has already realized that the flints are only the agents of a deeper reality, that they are the cause of many of the visions, "though not the cause of what lay behind the appearance—the *noumenon*; the thing itself" (Chapter XXVIII, p. 417). Saltfleet's action ethic, his awareness of his "false mortal state" in "the chains of the body" (Chapter XXVIII, p. 409), combined with his sensitivity and intellect, give him the capability to survive the joining of the stones.

In a thunderous climax that defies summary, Arsinal joins together the two halves of the stone and dies from the effect of the mystical forces released. Ingrid has a vision of the creation of life (described in musical metaphors) and comes to realize that the Great Mother consists of a trinity of anguish, sacrifice, and love (Chapter XXXIII, p. 473)—which calls to mind the trinity of feeling, relation, and existence in *A Voyage to Arcturus*. But both she and Saltfleet come to realize that this trinity, and indeed the Mother herself, only represent the coming into the world of something far more ancient, called "the ancient Ghost" or simply "the Ancient," which existed as a lonely unity before the beginning of time. The Great Mother represents the worldly Demiurge of this Ancient, and the "two great instincts of mankind"—the tendency to society and the tendency to spiritual isolation—derive respectively from the Demiurge and the Ancient. A few visionaries in man's history have striven to return to the Ancient, but the only way to do so is through its worldly manifestation, the Great Mother. Now the Great Mother has determined to create a new race, and Ingrid and Saltfleet are to serve as its Joseph and Mary

(Ingrid thinks often of Mary in these final pages). But the new race that Ingrid begins will not bring utopia: like the earlier race of Nordic warriors, it will initially bring discord and death to the world. "She must be mother, too, of horrors and madnesses, men shattered, women demented, children starved and orphaned, the skies never silent for the ascending sounds of the undone" (Chapter XXXIII, p. 481). There will be no human love between her and Saltfleet, but rather the agony of serving a higher will, and "the child should be from their two agonies, and not from themselves" (Chapter XXXIII, p. 480). Ingrid tells Saltfleet she will go live in the far north, and he accompanies her from the Tor.

Many things in *Devil's Tor* seem directly in contradiction to the ideas expressed in *A Voyage to Arcturus*, and Lindsay himself wrote that "Between the philosophies of *Arcturus* and *Devil's Tor* there seems to be a chasm of contradiction."[5] In place of both Crystalman and Muspel, we have the overriding figure of the Great Mother; in place of a final vision of solitude, we have a vision of union and creation. Lindsay hoped to resolve these apparent contradictions in his unfinished final novel, *The Witch*, but as he himself knew, the contradictions are more apparent than real. In all three novels we have discussed thus far, there has been a continuing theme that the world has become decadent and impure, and that we can regain some sense of the deeper reality of things by returning to a younger world. Tormance is described as a "young world," in which the manifestations of the will are still apparent; Ulf's world of *The Haunted Woman* is likewise a world of youth and springtime that enables us to see beneath the encrustations of illusion imposed by society and personality; the "purer" world of the ancient Nordic races is to be regained by the union of Ingrid and Saltfleet in *Devil's Tor*. One could perhaps find in all this a psychological striving for the purer world of perceptions represented by a lost childhood or a philosophical urge to find the roots of a phenomenology in some absolute *ding an sich*. Whatever the bases of Lindsay's particular fiction, however—whether it be the philosophies of Schopenhauer and Nietzsche in *Arcturus*, Celtic legends in *The Haunted Woman*, or the Great Mother myth in *Devil's Tor*—this striving to express a deeper reality remains a constant. It is unfortunate that in *Devil's Tor*, which may contain more of Lindsay's ideas than any other work, the sluggishness of the plot and the ponderousness of the style (several sentences run to nearly 150 words and read like a Henry James translation of Kant) make almost impossible demands on the reader and obscure what should be one of the most provocative works of philosophical fantasy of the twentieth century.

Notes

1. Quoted in J. B. Pick, "A Sketch of Lindsay's Life as Man and Writer," in *The Strange Genius of David Lindsay* (London: John Baker, 1970), p. 28.
2. *Devil's Tor* (London: Putnam's, 1932), Chapter VI, p. 70—Future references will be to the edition.
3. Quoted in Pick, "Sketch," *Strange Genius . . .*, p. 21.
4. Erich Neumann, *The Great Mother: An Analysis of the Archetype*, trans. Ralph Manheim (Princeton: Princeton University Press, 1963), p. 260.
5. Quoted in Pick, "Sketch," *Strange Genius . . .*, p. 30.

OTHER WORKS

Lindsay published two other novels during his lifetime, completed a third but was unable to find a publisher for it, and left a fourth unfinished. In addition, he left a series of *Philosophical Notes* which he probably did not intend to publish, but which offer many insights into his thinking and which now reside in the Scottish National Library.[1]

Of the two other novels published during his lifetime, *Sphinx* was the earlier, appearing in 1923, only a year after *The Haunted Woman*. In conception, it comes closer to traditional science-fiction than anything else Lindsay was to write. The "other world" of deeper reality, represented by Muspel in *Arcturus* and Ulf's world in *The Haunted Woman*, is here much closer to home: it is the world of dreams. Nicholas Cabot, Lindsay's protagonist, explains that in certain dreams, which we cannot remember upon awaking, we catch a glimpse of the deeper reality that surrounds us, of the truth in human relations. To test this hypothesis, Cabot is trying to develop a machine to record dreams. While he is working on it, he moves into the home of a family called the Sturts, who live in an isolated village. There he becomes involved, in varying degrees, with three women: Evelyn, a daughter of the family; Celia Hantish, a pretty neighborhood widow to whom he becomes engaged; and Lore Jensen, a composer who has been reduced to writing sentimental songs to support herself. Lore in many ways is the central figure in the book—one cannot help but wonder if her predicament is based on Lindsay's own growing feeling that he had to write "down" to his audiences—and it is one of her musical compositions that gives the book its title. The piece is called "Sphinx," and in reading its description one cannot help but think of *A Voyage to Arcturus*:

> One could almost see the burning sand of the desert and feel the enervating sunshine. By degrees, the theme became more troubled and passionate, quietly in the beginning, but with a gradually rising storm—not physical, but of emotion—until everything was like an unsteady sea of menace and terror. Towards the end, crashing dissonances appeared, but just when he was expecting the conventional climax to come, all the theme threads united in a sudden quietening, which almost at once took shape as an indubitable *question*. It could then be seen that all that had gone before had been leading the way to this question, and that what had appeared simple and understandable had been really nothing of the sort, but, on the contrary, something very mysterious and profound. . . .[2]

By recording and playing back his own dreams, Nicholas comes to realize that Lore is suffering some immense agony, perhaps related to her inability to compose the music she wants, perhaps related to her involvement with a local character called Ferreira, who is in love with her. Lore eventually marries a music critic, but she later commits suicide by drowning herself in a deep stream. After Lore's death, Evelyn makes a recording of a dream of her father, Sturt, and the dream reveals that through death, Lore has been able to liberate her "other self." Nicholas also appears in this dream, and the dream ends with he and Lore riding off across the sea on horseback. Realizing the implications of this, Evelyn rushes to Nicholas's room, but finds him dead.

The notion of a man and woman fundamentally attracted to one another, but separated by their own surface personalities and social conventions, recalls *The Haunted Woman*, and the idea of their finally being united in some other world calls to mind not only that novel, but also *Devil's Tor*, *The Violet Apple*, and *The Witch*. Colin Wilson complains that *Sphinx*, with its portrayal of the petty intrigues and gossip of an English village, suffers from "a pervading atmosphere of triviality,"[3] but one might argue that the masks of social convention represented by such pettiness became of increasing concern to Lindsay, and that this sort of behavior is described in some form or another in all his books—even in *A Voyage to Arcturus*, with its opening social gathering at a seance.

The charge of triviality has been more consistently and seriously brought to bear against the novel that Lindsay published three years after *Sphinx*. *The Adventures of M. de Mailly* (1926) is a complex account of social and political intrigues at the court of Louis the Fourteenth and is the only novel of Lindsay's to contain no element of fantasy. Compared to Lindsay's other works, *de Mailly* was relatively successful; in 1927, retitled *Blade for Sale*, it became the first of his works to appear in the United States. Colin Wilson, J. B. Pick, and E. H. Visiak pretty generally dismiss the novel as a "potboiler" written solely as an entertainment and to raise money, but J. Derrick McClure, in an article in *Studies in Scottish Literature*, makes an interesting case for regarding it as among the mainstream of Lindsay's writing.[4] McClure argues that the themes of illusion and self-deception, particularly in regard to social behavior, are as much a part of this novel as of Lindsay's fantasies—hence the setting in the court of Louis the Fourteenth, "where social ceremonial was developed to a degree rarely surpassed."[5] The novel consists of four episodes concerning an ingenious and witty courtier named de Mailly, whose complex schemes and whose understanding of people's capacity to be tricked by their own illusions enable him to survive in a world of unrelenting intrigue and betrayal. The complex of false assumptions, mistaken identities, coincidences, cross-purposes, schemes, treacheries, and the like that go to make up the plot at once parody such authors as Dumas and raise their art to a level of remarkable ingenuity.

At the time *de Mailly* was published, Lindsay was completing revisions on *The Violet Apple*, a novel he had been unable to publish two years earlier and one of two novels that were not to see print during Lindsay's lifetime. *The Violet Apple* continues the now-familiar theme of two people, a man and a woman, kept apart by social conventions and comintiments to others, who are finally brought together through some mystical force and for some higher purpose. As in *Devil's Tor*, Lindsay makes use of a familiar myth to symbolize this higher force—in this case the myth of the garden of Eden. Anthony Kerr, the playwright-protagonist, is perhaps the closest we have seen yet to a self-portrait of Lindsay in his work:

> He had a deep mystical bent; his thoughts, doubtless, were way above the heads of the theatrical crowd, but he had conceived the happy expedient of introducing fantastic entities to his pieces to relieve the drab monotony of the characters and manners of the modern world. . . . it was a great test of artistry and brought out the best of his intelligence to translate his secret philosophy into concrete shapes of fun and mockery, which a more educated generation hereafter might appreciate at their proper worth. Not to go too closely into his creed, he soberly regarded mankind, with all its boasted skill, energy, science, law, and progress, as no more than a petty heap of blind, wriggling, three-dimensional insect-like beings, surrounded by terrific unseen forces . . . We were separated from a whole active universe by an opaque wall of senselessness.
>
> He brought no heavy guns to bear in his work. He introduced his extravagant figures, and left them at that. But since they were the equivalent of his theories, it necessarily followed that his art was cynical in underlying essence, inasmuch as he deliberately regulated his fancies to meet the assumed level of his audience, whom, accordingly, he at once flattered and despised.[6]

(Perhaps in a stroke of wishful thinking, Lindsay makes Kerr into a successful playwright.)

Kerr inherits from his aunt an ancient glass figure of a snake, supposedly brought back from the crusades, with an apple seed imbedded in it that, according to legend, came from the original tree in Eden. The glass figure is accidentally shattered, and, as something of a joke, Kerr plants the seed. From it grows a small, deformed apple tree, which dies immediately after producing four tiny violet apples. Kerr is engaged to a rather vapid young lady named Grace Lytham, whose brother Jim is engaged to the sensitive and mystical Haidee Croyland. Needless to say, the *real* relationship is to be between Anthony and Haidee, and their shared confidences begin to generate suspicion on the part of their respective partners. The culmination of the action occurs when Haidee and Anthony each eat of the violet apples and behold visions of one another as divinities, perhaps destined to create a new race as Ingrid and Saltfleet are in *Devil's Tor*. Finally realizing the inevitability of their union, they break off their respective engagements. Perhaps more consistently permeated by Christian imagery than any of his other works (including the striking image of a grove of trees, which appears first in a painting and later in reality, through which the sky appears to assume the shape of a cross), *The Violet Apple* is in many ways even more slight and elliptical than *The Haunted Woman* and does not really add substantially to our understanding of Lindsay's thought.

The Witch, however, is another matter. Lindsay worked on this last novel throughout much of the thirties and apparently intended it to be the definitive treatment of the same basic story he had used in *The Haunted Woman, Devil's Tor,* and *The Violet Apple*. It was also to offer a summing-up of his philosophy of love and sexuality, resolving and synthesizing many of the apparent contradictions between *Arcturus* and *Devil's Tor*, his two major earlier works. The novel even seems to return to the spirit of *Arcturus* in its eccentric nomenclature: the central characters are Ragnar Pole and Urda Noett. Lindsay could hardly have concocted names more suggestive of the north, of ancientness, and of the twilight of the gods.

Pole seems to be another self-portrait, only this time a harsher and more despairing one. He is a writer whose works are "read by few, comprehended by fewer, wanted by none."[7] At a social gathering, which opens the novel, Pole feels a strange psychic "disturbance" from Urda and vows to meet her. But when he goes to talk to her, she is with a strange man named Bluewright, a death-like figure. Ragnar does not interrupt, but later he learns that no one else at the party knows of Bluewright or had seen him talking with Urda. Gaspary, a friend of Ragnar's, suggests that Urda is a witch and offers an involved argument defending his use of this term. Throughout history, he says, civilization has advanced on a purely material level through the work of scientists and inventors, whose work has addressed itself only to the surfaces of things. Against these minds has worked a tradition of "wise women" who have preserved the knowledge of a deeper reality, who have thus been called witches and ostracized and who have come in the popular mind to be associated with hysterics and charlatans. "The witch has been an unsocial type," explains Gaspary. "She has set herself against the journey of civilization . . . the journey ending in a prison."

Aided by a woman named Faustine, Ragnar searches for Urda's home, Morion House, an ancient structure on the site of a ninth-century battle where a mysterious and powerful Anglo-Saxon chief—whose name translates as Bluewright—was supposedly killed. This legend is told to Ragnar by another mysterious character—Captain Flint, whom Ragnar had believed dead for many years and who subsequently disappears again. Like the observatory in *Arcturus*, Ulf's tower in *The Haunted Woman*, and Devil's Tor in *Devil's Tor*, Morion House is the portal to another world—called in this novel heaven. Urda, then, is a "woman of heaven," but it is clear that this heaven is closer to Muspel than to any traditional Christian conception.

After reaching Morion House ("Morion" is translated as "sea-witch-wood"), Ragnar enters a darkened hallway and soon finds himself in a dream-like landscape that comes closer to the visionary power of *Arcturus* than anything in Lindsay's later works. Here he meets Faustine, who says, " 'I am the world' " and who explains to Ragnar that he is to experience the journey of the soul after death. He will pass through three "musics":

" 'The first music is passion, the second rests on the passion, but itself is calmness. The third, I think, is the soul's longest journey through heavens and spaces, to its own wisdom of loneliness.' " Like Dante's Virgil, Faustine can only guide Ragnar for part of this journey. She seems to represent will: after transcending will, or passion, the soul passes into nothingness (the Muspel of *Arcturus*), finally achieving a higher plane of being (as represented by the Great Mother in *Devil's Tor* and the now-divine figure of Urda in this novel). Thus Lindsay apparently hoped to unite the visions of *Arcturus* and *Devil's Tor* into a single, all-encompassing vision of transcendence. But we cannot be sure, for what remains of the manuscript ends here.

The Witch is almost as difficult to read as *Devil's Tor*, and like that earlier novel it is full of lengthy passages of introspection and meditation on the nature of love, both as a force within the world and a force for transcending the world; on the meaning and nature of the Ancient; on the role of the Ancient and the Great Mother in history and psychology; on the role of illusion in life; and so on. More than that earlier novel, however, it shows that Lindsay's philosophy does not end with *A Voyage to Arcturus,* that the apparent process of world-negating that goes on in that novel was intended by its author to be merely a prelude to something else, that there was indeed a story yet to be told after Krag and Nightspore set off into the dark waters at the end of that novel. In many ways, Lindsay's problem was not unlike Dante's in writing the *Commedia:* the Inferno is striking, dramatic, and relatively easy to portray; but paradise, the positive vision that follows the negative, is a far more difficult concept to explain.

Notes

1. Information contained in a letter from J. B. Pick, 15 September 1978.
2. Quoted in Colin Wilson, "Lindsay as Novelist and Mystic," in *The Strange Genius of David Lindsay* (London: John Baker, 1970), p. 70. Since I have been unable to locate a copy of this novel, I have relied largely on Wilson's account.
3. Wilson, p. 71.
4. J. Derrick McClure, " 'Purely as Entertainment'? *Adventures of Monsieur de Mailly* as a Representative Work of David Lindsay," *Studies in Scottish Literature*, 11 (1974), pp. 226–236.
5. Ibid., p. 229.
6. Quoted from the typescript. *The Violet Apple* and *The Witch*, edited by J. B. Pick, were published in one volume in 1976 by the Chicago Review Press.
7. This and subsequent quotations are taken from the typescript.

VII
PRIMARY BIBLIOGRAPHY

The Adventures of M. de Mailly. First edition: London: Melrose, 1926; Reprint [as *Blade for Sale*] : New York: McBride, 1927.

Devil's Tor. London: Putnam's, 1932. Reprint: New York: Arno Press, 1978.

The Haunted Woman. London: Methuen, 1922. Reprints: London: Gollancz, 1964; Hollywood, California: Newcastle, 1975.

Sketch Notes for a New System of Philosophy. Unpublished; in Scottish National Library.

Sphinx. London: John Long, 1923.

The Violet Apple and The Witch. Ed. J. B. Pick. Chicago: Chicago Review Press, 1976. Reprint: London: Sidgwich & Jackson, 1978.

A Voyage to Arcturus. London: Methuen, 1920. Reprints: London: Gollancz, 1946, 1963, 1968; New York: Macmillan, 1963; New York: Ballantine, 1968, 1973 [paperback] ; Boston: Gregg Press, 1977 [photographic reprint of 1st ed.] . (For introductions to these volumes, see secondary bibliography.)

VIII
ANNOTATED SECONDARY BIBLIOGRAPHY

Amis, Kingsley. "Adventures on a Distant Star" (rev. of *A Voyage to Arcturus). New York Times Book Review*, 24 November 1963, p. 60. Some valid criticisms, but chiefly useful as an indication of the sort of reviews *Arcturus* has consistently received.

Eiseley, Loren. "Introduction" to *A Voyage to Arcturus.* New York: Macmillan, 1963, pp. vii-x. This brief introduction, reprinted in the Ballantine edition of the novel, is sympathetic but misleading, and contains factual errors.

Lewis, C. S. "On Stories," in *Of Other Worlds: Essays and Stories.* Ed. Walter Hooper. New York: Harcourt, Brace, & World, 1966, pp. 3-21. Contains a brief discussion of *Arcturus*, praising it for its "lived dialectic."

McClure, J. Derrick. "*Devil's Tor*: A Rehabilitation of David Lindsay's 'Monster.'" *Extrapolation*, 21, 4 (Winter 1980), 367-378. Explores the difficulties in reading *Devil's Tor* and argues its significance.

—————. " 'Purely as Entertainment'? *Adventures of Monsieur de Mailly* as a Representative Work of David Lindsay." *Studies in Scottish Literature*, 11 (1974), 226-236. Argues that the deceptions and intrigue of *de Mailly* are consistent with Lindsay's broader themes of illusion and self-deception; also briefly discusses other novels.

Mensing, Van A. "Introduction" to *A Voyage to Arcturus.* Boston: Gregg Press, 1977, pp. v-xvii. The most complete exposition to date of the debt *Arcturus* owes to Nietzsche.

Pick, J. B. "The Work of David Lindsay." *Studies in Scottish Literature*,

1 (1964), 171-182. General essay represents an early attempt to revive the study of Lindsay.

Pohl, Joy. "Dualities in David Lindsay's *A Voyage to Arcturus.*" *Extrapolation*, 22, 2 (Summer 1981), 164-170. A reading of *Arcturus* based on thematic oppositions.

Rabkin, Eric S. "Conflation of Genres and Myths in David Lindsay's *A Voyage to Arcturus.*" *The Journal of Narrative Technique*, 7 (1977), 149-55. Analyzes *A Voyage to Arcturus* as a blending of science-fiction episodes and an overall fantasy structure that uses fantasy to extend science-fiction into the realm of serious myth.

————. *The Fantastic in Literature.* Princeton: Princeton University Press, 1976. Discusses *Arcturus* as an example of how "escape" literature may have a serious purpose.

Russ, Joanna. "Dream-Literature and Science Fiction." *Extrapolation*, 11 (1969), 6-14. Cites *Arcturus* as an example of adolescent "dream-literature," inferior to better science-fiction.

Schofield, Jack. "Cosmic Imagery in *A Voyage to Arcturus.*" *Extrapolation*, 13 (1972), 146-151. Reply to Russ defends *Arcturus* and points out interesting parallels to Dante and others.

Scholes, Robert, and Eric S. Rabkin. *Science-Fiction: History, Science, Vision.* New York: Oxford University Press, 1977. pp. 207-212 discuss *Arcturus* as a "representative" science-fiction novel.

Sellin, Bernard. *The Life and Works of David Lindsay,* translated by Kenneth Gunnell. Cambridge: Cambridge University Press, 1981. The first scholarly biography of Lindsay and the longest sustained critical discussion of his works to date; originally a doctoral thesis at the Sorbonne.

Visiak, E. H. "The Arcturan Shadow." *Notes and Queries*, 178 (1940), 225-227. The earliest critical appreciation of Lindsay; draws Miltonic parallels.

————. "Introduction" to *A Voyage to Arcturus.* London: Gollancz, 1963. Repeats many of the ideas of Visiak's 1940 essay.

Wilson, Colin. *Eagle and Earwig.* London: John Baker, 1966. A chapter on *Arcturus* mostly recounts Wilson's experiences with the novel.

————. Wilson, Colin. *The Haunted Man: The Strange Genius of David Lindsay.* San Bernardino, Cal.: Borgo Press, 1979. With the exception of a brief new discussion of *The Haunted Woman,* essentially a reprint of Wilson's essay in *The Strange Genius of David Lindsay* (see below).

————., E. H. Visiak, and J. B. Pick. *The Strange Genius of David Lindsay.* London: John Baker, 1970. A collection of essays and reminiscences that is the major source of information on Lindsay, but contains little critical perspective.

Wolfe, Gary K. "David Lindsay and George MacDonald." *Studies in Scottish Literature*, 12 (1974), 131-145. Argues for MacDonald's influence on Lindsay and notes parallels between their careers.

————. "Symbolic Fantasy." *Genre*, 8 (1975), 194-209. Places Lindsay in a tradition of symbolic, rather than allegorical, fantasy.

www.ingramcontent.com/pod-product-compliance
Lightning Source LLC
Chambersburg PA
CBHW021349090426
42742CB00008B/788